DEAD BOYS 1977

The Lost Photographs of Dave Treat

Dead Boys 1977: The Lost Photographs of Dave Treat
First edition 2017

ISBN: 978-0-578-19073-0

Edited and designed by Ron Kretsch

"On Becoming" by Brittany M. Hudak was originally published in a slightly different form in the 2105 book *STIV:1976*

Photos printed and digitized by Bryon Miller

Many thanks to Cheetah Chrome, Johnny Blitz, Jimmy Zero, Lynne Treat, Lenny Pansky, Kyle Pansky, John Petkovic, Marty Geramita, Ilka Erren Pardiñas, Martin Schneider, Tara McGinley and Richard Metzger of Dangerous Minds (www.dangerousminds.net) and Andy Leach of the Rock and Roll Hall of Fame and Museum Library and Archives

Printed in the USA
Signature Book Printing www.sbpbooks.com

deadboys1977.com

TO MY SON, JUSTIN

—Dave Treat

PART I: THE DEAD BOYS

INTRODUCTION

PUNK ROCK IS ONE OF ROCK 'N' ROLL'S GREATEST STORIES ever told, and the cultural shock of its ascendance is matched by its incredible durability as a template for rebellion. The British love to claim a London origin for the movement, an assertion made ridiculous by the indisputable fact of so many New York punk bands already existing when the UK was still in the midst of the Pub Rock movement. Calendars don't lie. But New York doesn't exactly deserve all the roses—Midwesterners led the charge. Late '60s Detroit had The Stooges, The MC5, and The Up, and shortly after, in unassuming, totally beat-up little early '70s Cleveland, Ohio, before anyone had ever heard of a "Ramone," serious freaks toiling away in total, blessed obscurity hatched an insurgency of unprecedentedly anti-social rock music that pointed the way forward.

In the beginning were the electric eels (lowercase on purpose) and Rocket From the Tombs. Both bands were utterly out of step with their times; loud, hateful, and assaultive in an era when James Taylor was becoming one of the best-selling singers in the world. It is Rocket that concerns us most here, for after one year of existence, that proto-punk band splintered into two very different but very important factions. The band's more art-wardly inclined members formed the formidable and still-extant Pere Ubu, while the band's rockers—drummer John "Johnny Blitz" Madansky and guitarist Eugene "Cheetah Chrome" O'Connor—joined with guitarist William "Jimmy Zero" Wilden and singer Steven "Stiv Bators" Bator to form the gutterally glammy Frankenstein.

Frankenstein only lasted a few months, but their existence was documented in a series of *amazing* concert photos (Chrome sporting shoulder-length hair, guyliner, and lipstick; Bators wearing sheer pantyhose instead of pants, leaving nothing to the imagination) and some blown-out-sounding recordings that were released in the mid-'90s as *Eve of the Dead Boys*. Perhaps realizing glam was a dead end that couldn't contain their energy, Frankenstein abandoned it to seek their own identity, ramping up their personal and musical unruliness and changing their name to The Dead Boys. That moment, that transition, is the accidental subject of the photos in this book.

Chrome and Bators lived and wrote music in an apartment on Giel Avenue in Lakewood. Their friend and fellow tenant, Dave Treat, was a photography student at the nearby (and now defunct) Cooper School of Art. In 1977, the newly rechristened Dead Boys needed promo photos, so they spent an afternoon with Treat, shooting in Downtown Cleveland around seedy Prospect Avenue, then an utter wasteland. You could see other humans in the few blocks between the Terminal Tower and the Woolworth's department store, but much of the rest of Downtown in the '70s could have damn near passed for Dresden in 1945. The band made that wasteland its playground. Treat's lens captured not just a rock band but a powerful portrait of the Rust Belt decay that wormed its way so unmistakably into The Dead Boys' music.

Treat had previously made Stiv the subject of his student portfolio, yielding an incredible session of intimate portraits of a young artist on the verge of a crowning achievement. But as it happened, despite the eventual importance of his subjects, only one of Treat's photos was ever published, an alley shot in an issue of *Rock Scene* magazine, a shot that would become famous only when it was re-created by Glenn Brown for the cover of the band's debut LP *Young Loud and Snotty*. The band relocated to New York, cut their hair, and added bassist Jeff Magnum, so Treat's photos were rendered obsolete, and into the proverbial shoebox they went, to finally be exhumed for exhibition almost forty years later. This book contains those shots, the Stiv portraits, and some of Treat's concert photos, including never-before-seen shots from The Dead Boys' 1977 Cleveland show opening for The Dictators. (Also on that bill: an opening band from Illinois called Cheap Trick.)

We've supplemented those historic photos with original commentary by two of the surviving band members themselves, Cheetah Chrome and Johnny Blitz, talking about music, Cleveland, Stiv, their beginnings, and each other. This is not an attempt at an oral history of the Dead Boys, or of punk rock—you can get that from *Please Kill Me*, *From the Velvets to the Voivoids,* or *Cheetah Chrome: A Dead Boy's Tale: From the Front Lines of Punk Rock*. Rather, this is the story of something more modest and intimate—an afternoon with four young guys from a forgotten place who were about to unleash something incredible.

—Ron Kretsch
Contributing Editor, Dangerous Minds
February 2017, Cleveland, Ohio

FOREWORD

IN 1976, I MOVED INTO AN APARTMENT IN LAKEWOOD on Giel Avenue. At the time, I was studying photography at Cooper School of Art. A few months later, Stiv Bator moved in next door and we became friends. Over the next year, hanging out with Stiv, Cheetah, Johnny, and Jimmy was always a great time. The parties on Giel Avenue were legendary. For details, when you can, read Cheetah's book *Cheetah Chrome: A Dead Boy's Tale: From the Front Lines of Punk Rock*. I would get home from school and Stiv would stop in and I got to know him really well. He agreed to be a subject for my final portfolio. When you got Stiv in front of a camera, what a subject he was! In May of 1977, Stiv and Cheetah asked me if I could shoot a promo photo of them. We spent the day in downtown Cleveland. The results are some of the photos in this book. I hope you enjoy them as much as I enjoyed taking them.

—Dave Treat
February 2017, Cleveland, Ohio

THE DEAD BOYS

L-R:

Stiv Bators (R.I.P. 1990)

Cheetah Chrome

Johnny Blitz

Jimmy Zero

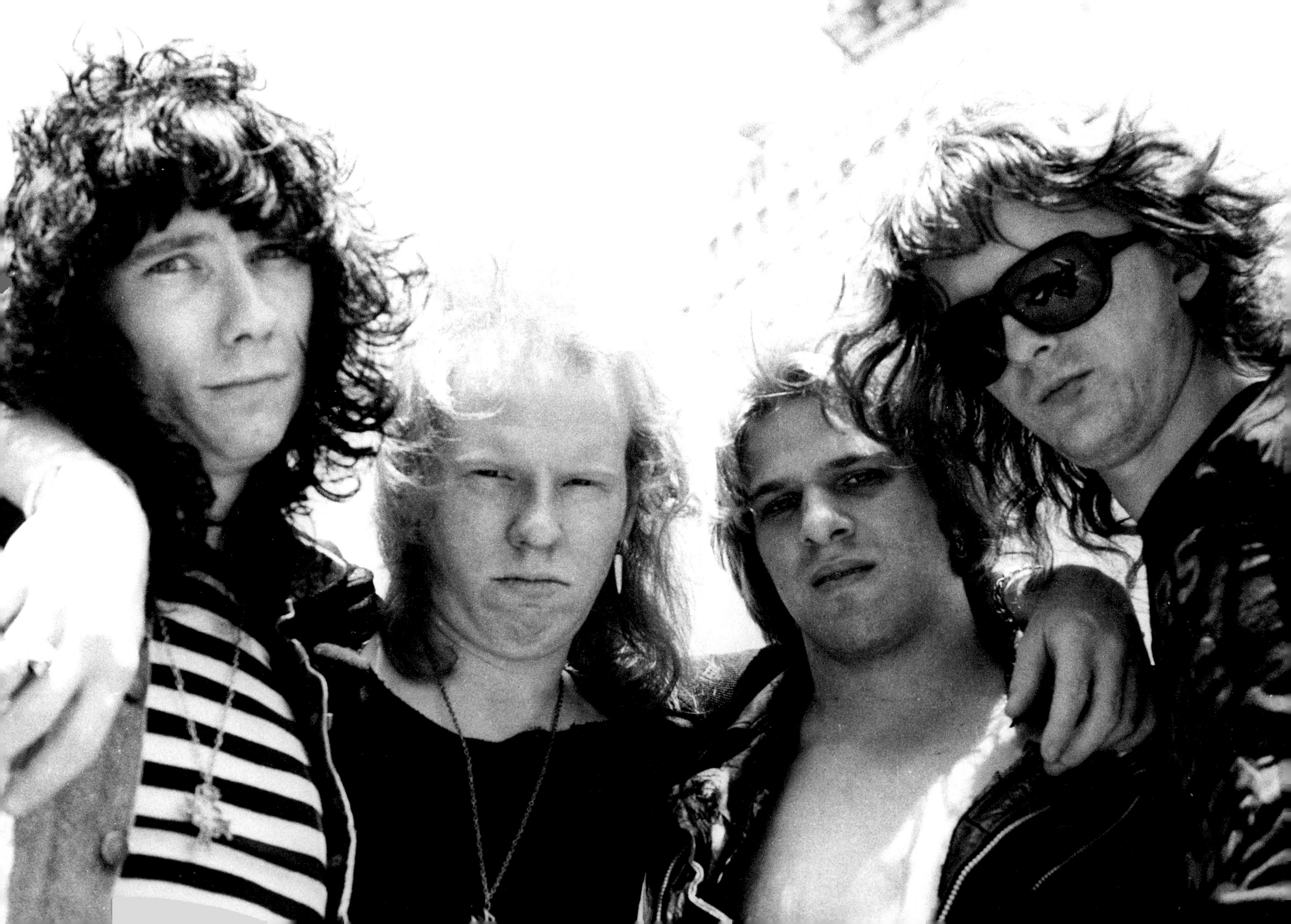

Cheetah Chrome:

We went to downtown Cleveland, by Prospect Avenue, for the pictures. We rehearsed there. And if you look at the picture that's like the *Young Loud and Snotty* cover shot, the building on the left is where we rehearsed.

Johnny Blitz:

I was really young, and I think that was my first photo shoot, and everyone was really pumped, really excited. I have no idea if those buildings are still there, but I'd really love to re-do that shot again with me, Jimmy, Jeff, and Cheetah. It'd be kinda cool, but you can't always go back.

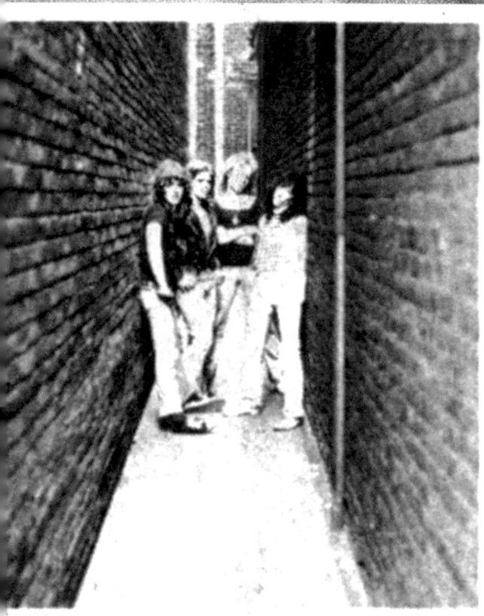

e Dead Boys, seen here being ıshed between two brick walls, ve been together for about six onths, and have only played Max's d CBGB's (not bad!) From left to ht: Jimmy Zero, Johnny Blitz, eetah Chrome, and Stiv Bators. u can write the Boys (via the Dead ter office??) at 222 E. 27th St., #12, Y.C., N.Y. 10016. (Pic: David Treat)

Scene magazine, May 1977

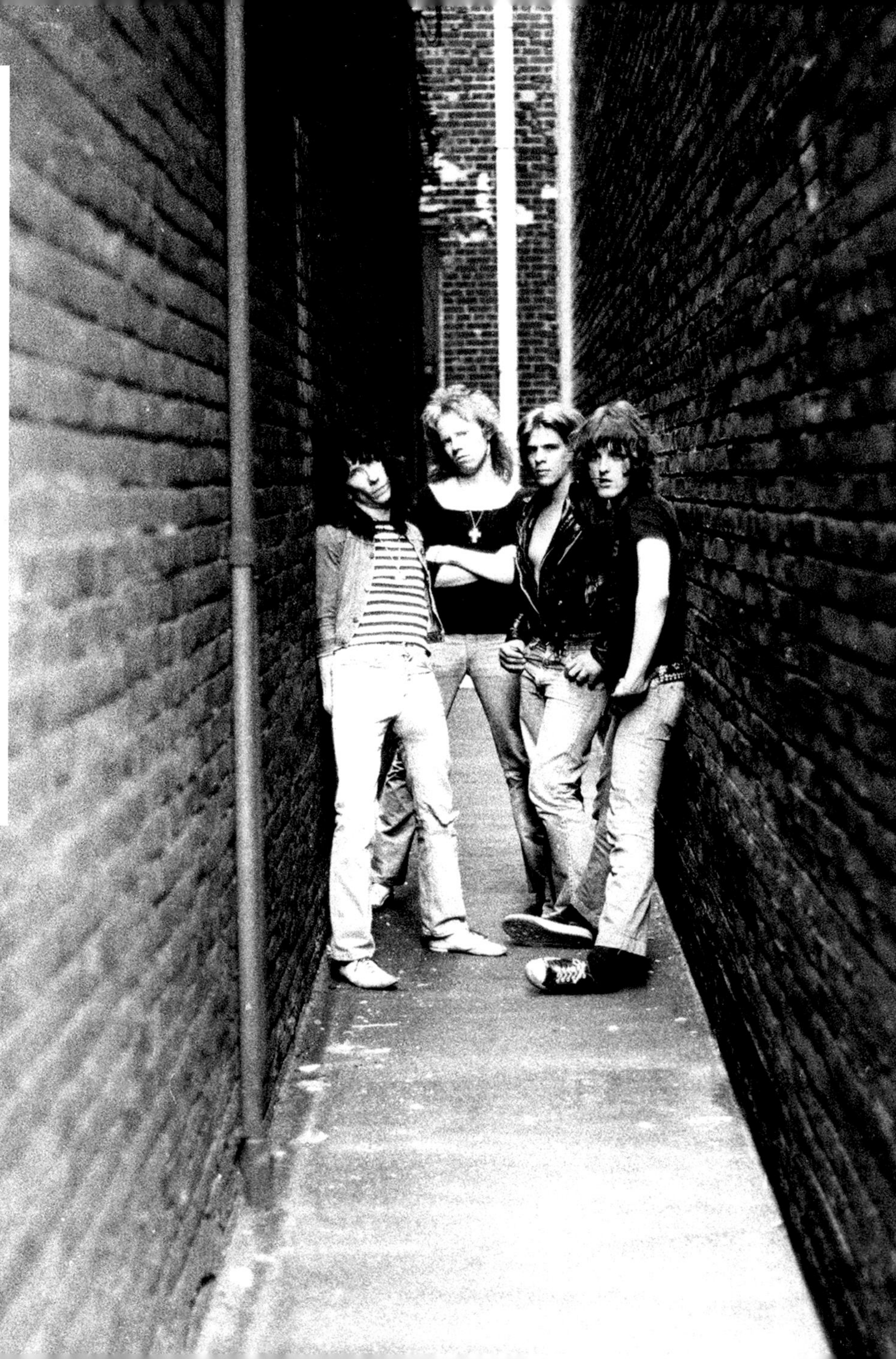

Young Loud and Snotty photo by Glenn Brown, 1977

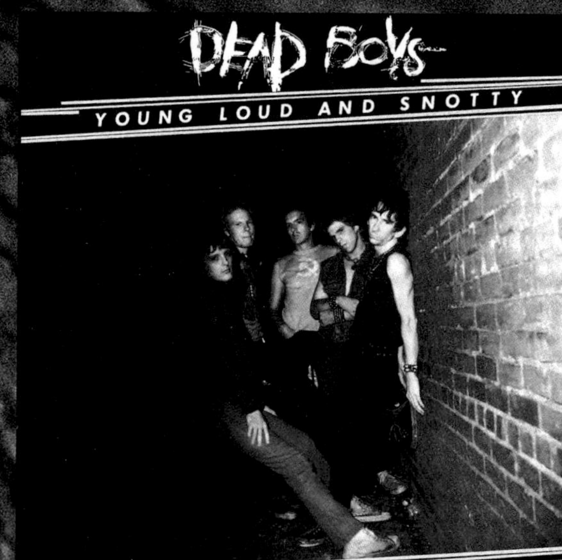

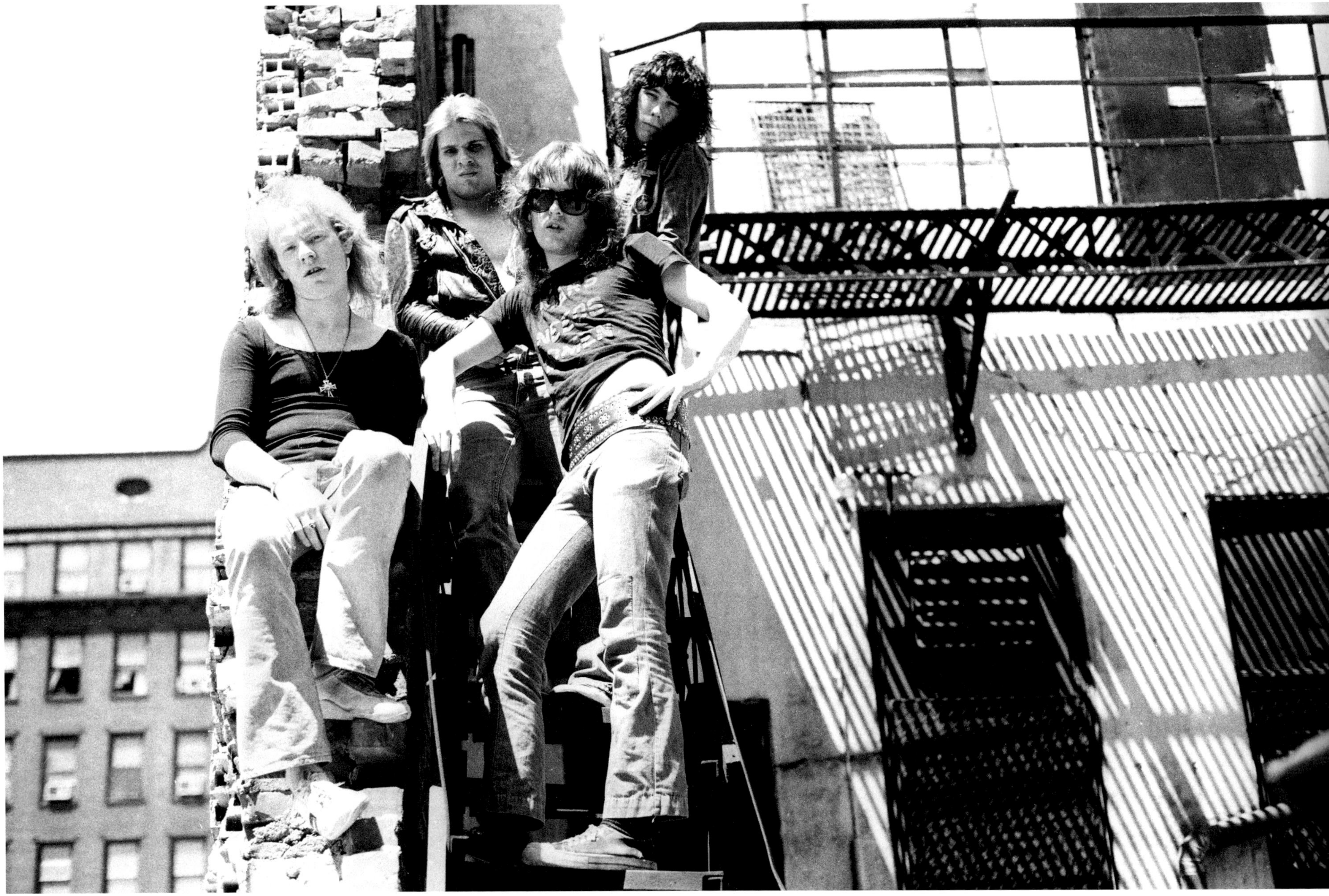

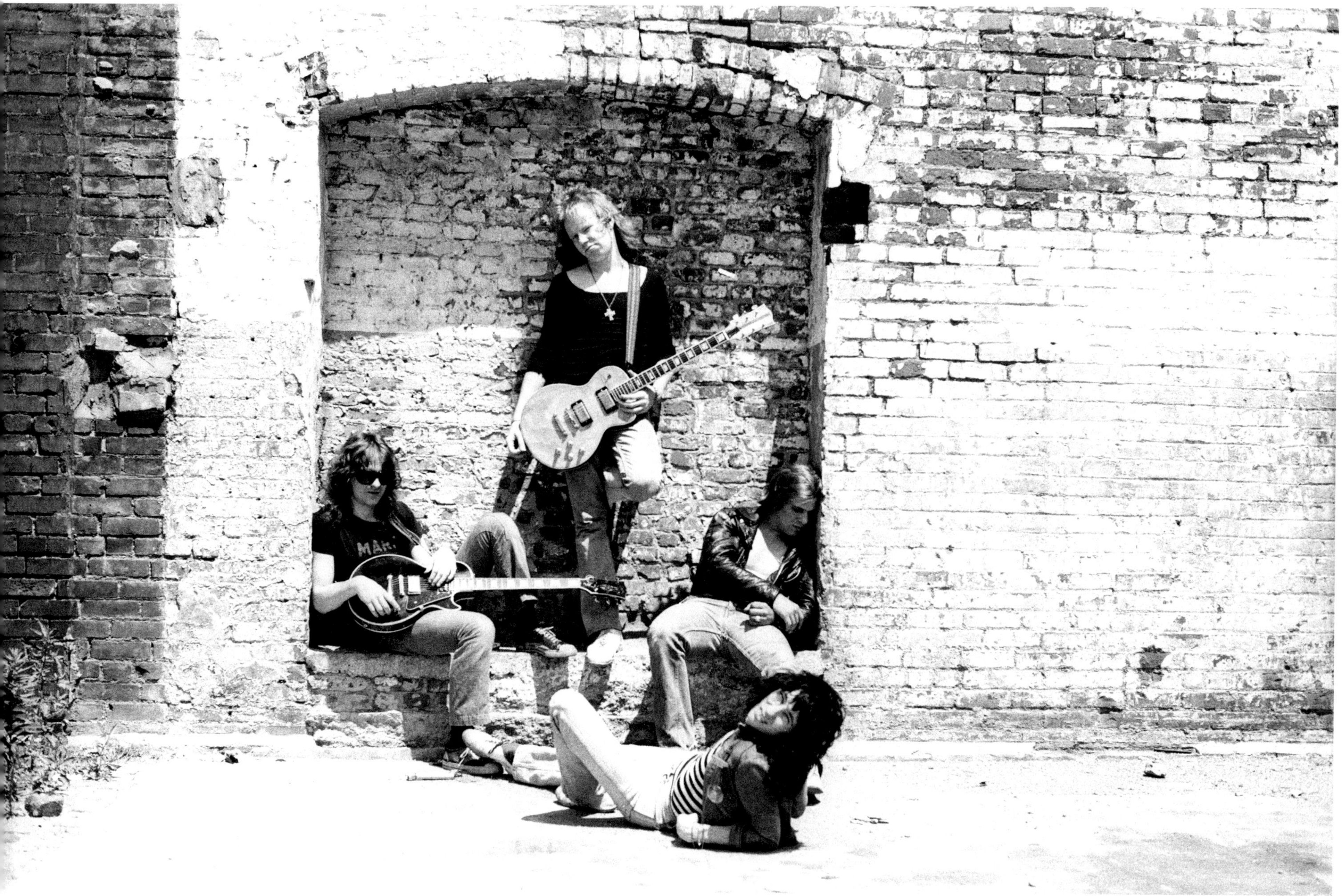

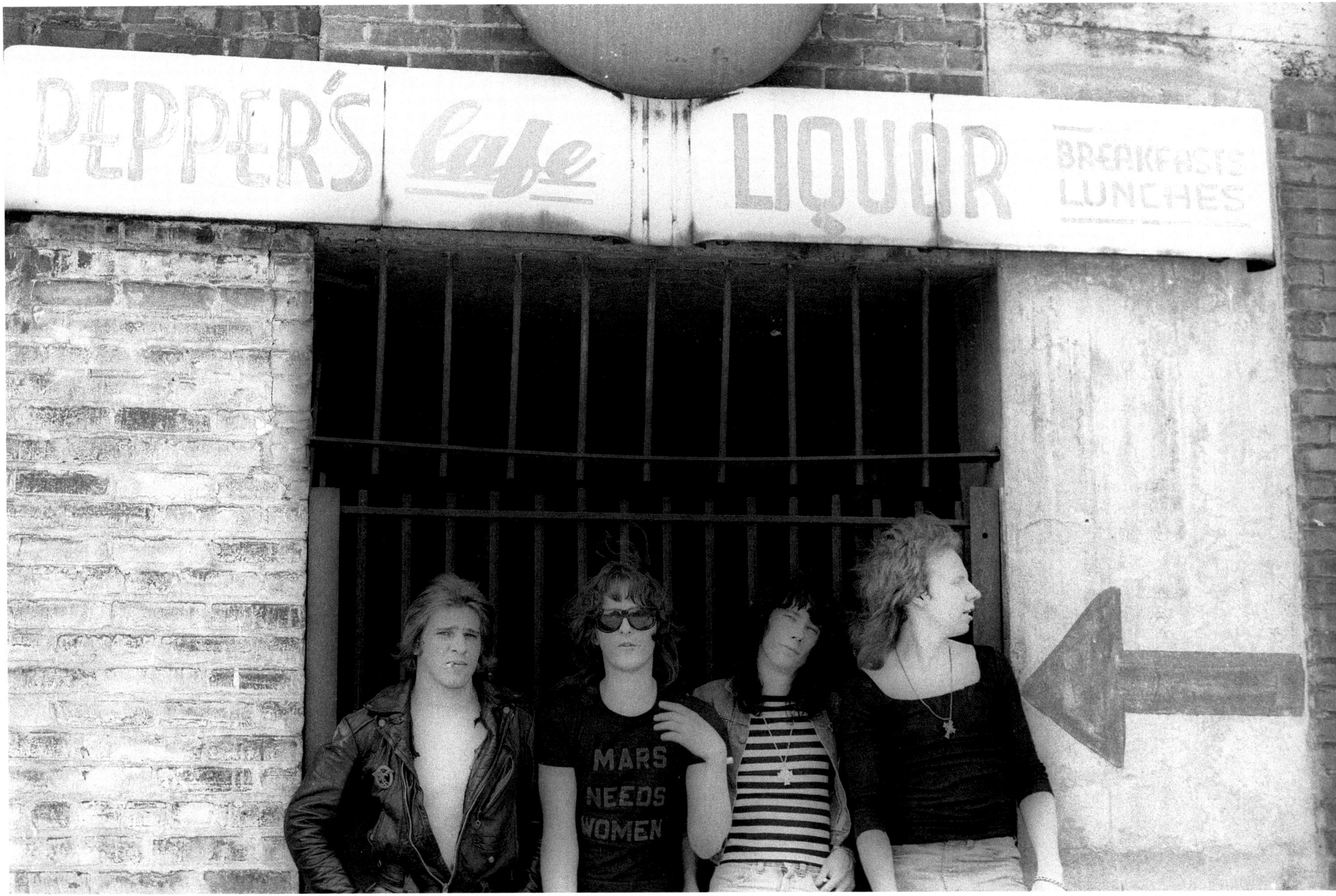
PEPPER'S
Cafe
LIQUOR
BREAKFASTS
LUNCHES
MARS
NEEDS
WOMEN

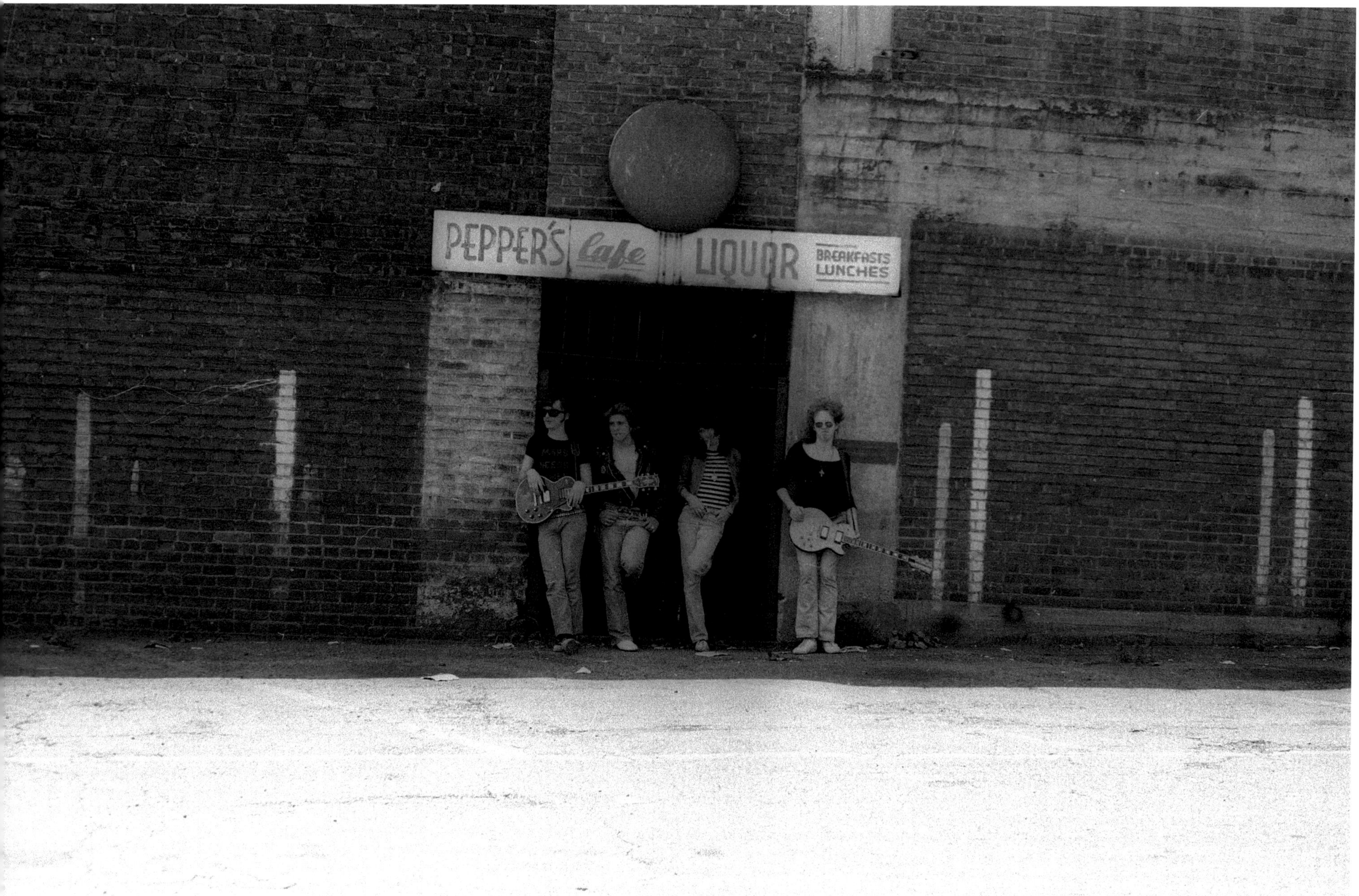
PEPPER'S
Cafe
LIQUOR
BREAKFASTS
LUNCHES

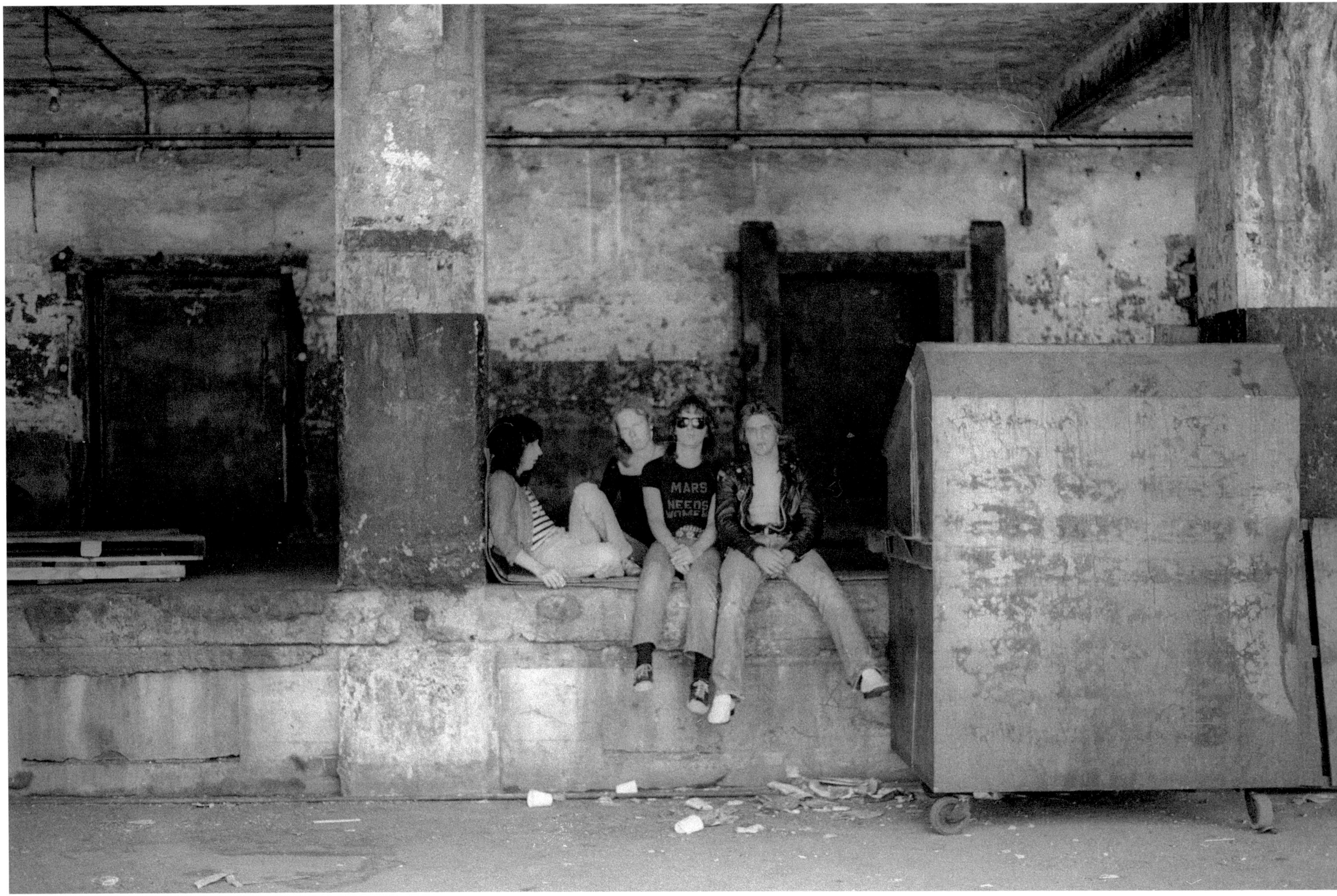
MARS
NEEDS

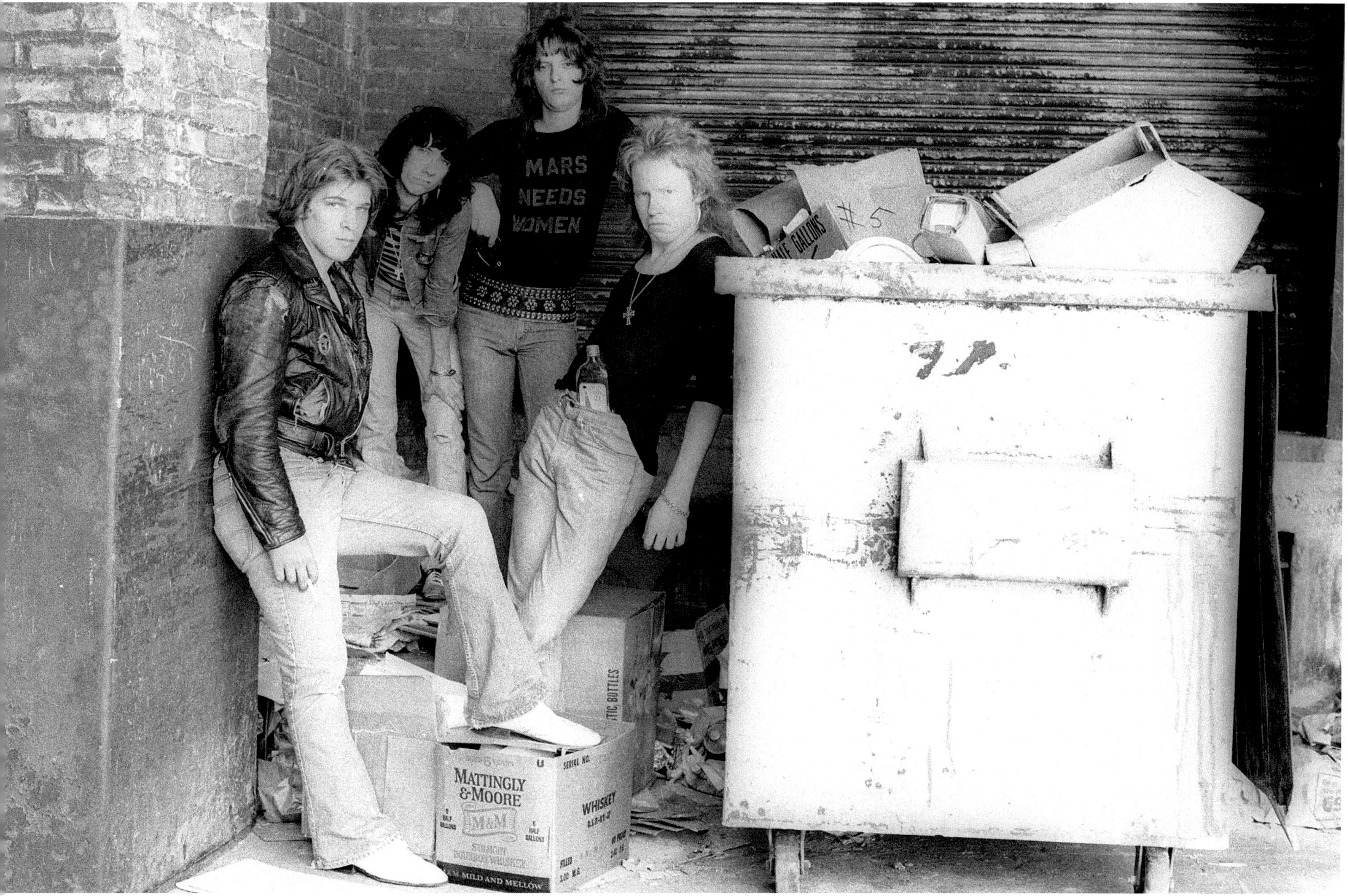
MARS
NEEDS
WOMEN
#5
MATTINGLY
&MOORE
M&M
WHISKEY
SERIAL NO.
MILD AND MELLOW

Cheetah Chrome:

Back then, Cleveland looked like a neutron bomb went off, all these big buildings, and like twelve people walking around. It was really kind of desolate. There was traffic, but not much, and there was hardly anybody on the streets, so we were able to just like walk down the middle of the streets, stop, take pictures, moon the camera, do whatever the hell we wanted to, and nobody would notice.

Johnny Blitz:

It was pretty wild walking around doing this. Big adventure downtown, right? We were looking for places to take good shots, and we were going off of what the Ramones had done—"Hey, there's a brick wall, there's another brick wall." So we were fishing for that kind of thing, and in Downtown Cleveland there were LOTS of those kinds of decayed old buildings. It was a bonanza.

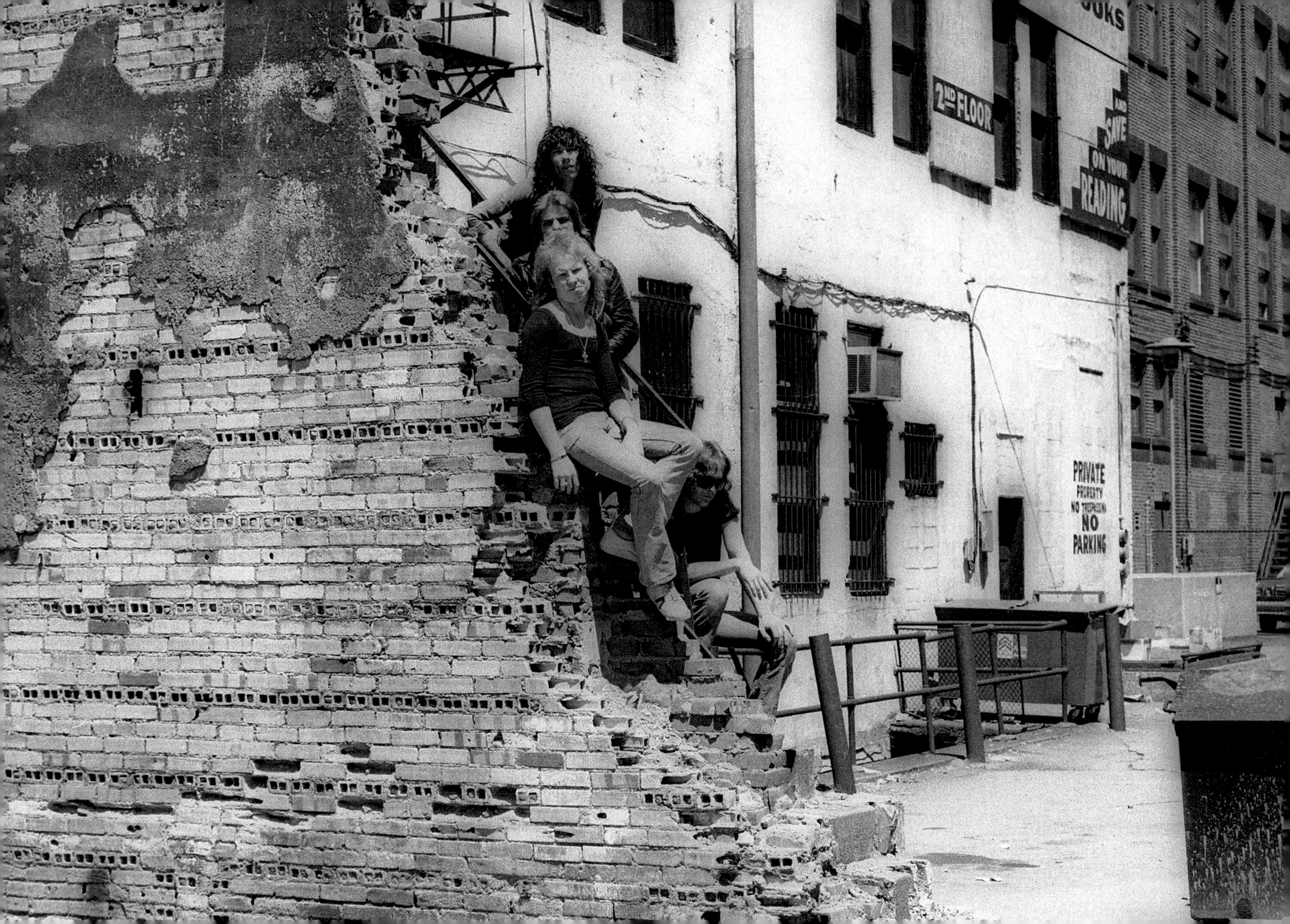
2ND FLOOR
AND SAVE ON YOUR READING
PRIVATE PROPERTY
NO TRESPASSING
NO PARKING

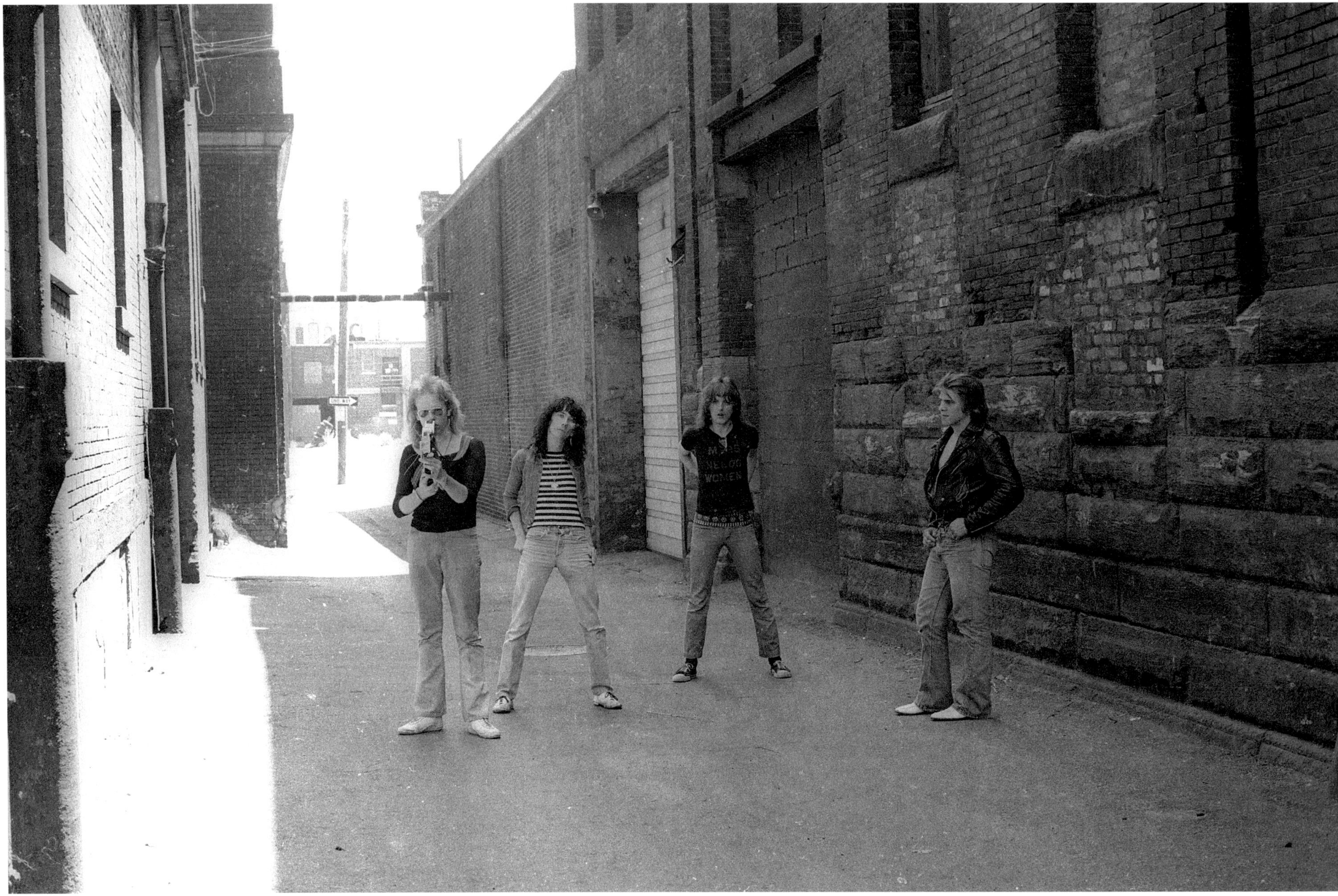

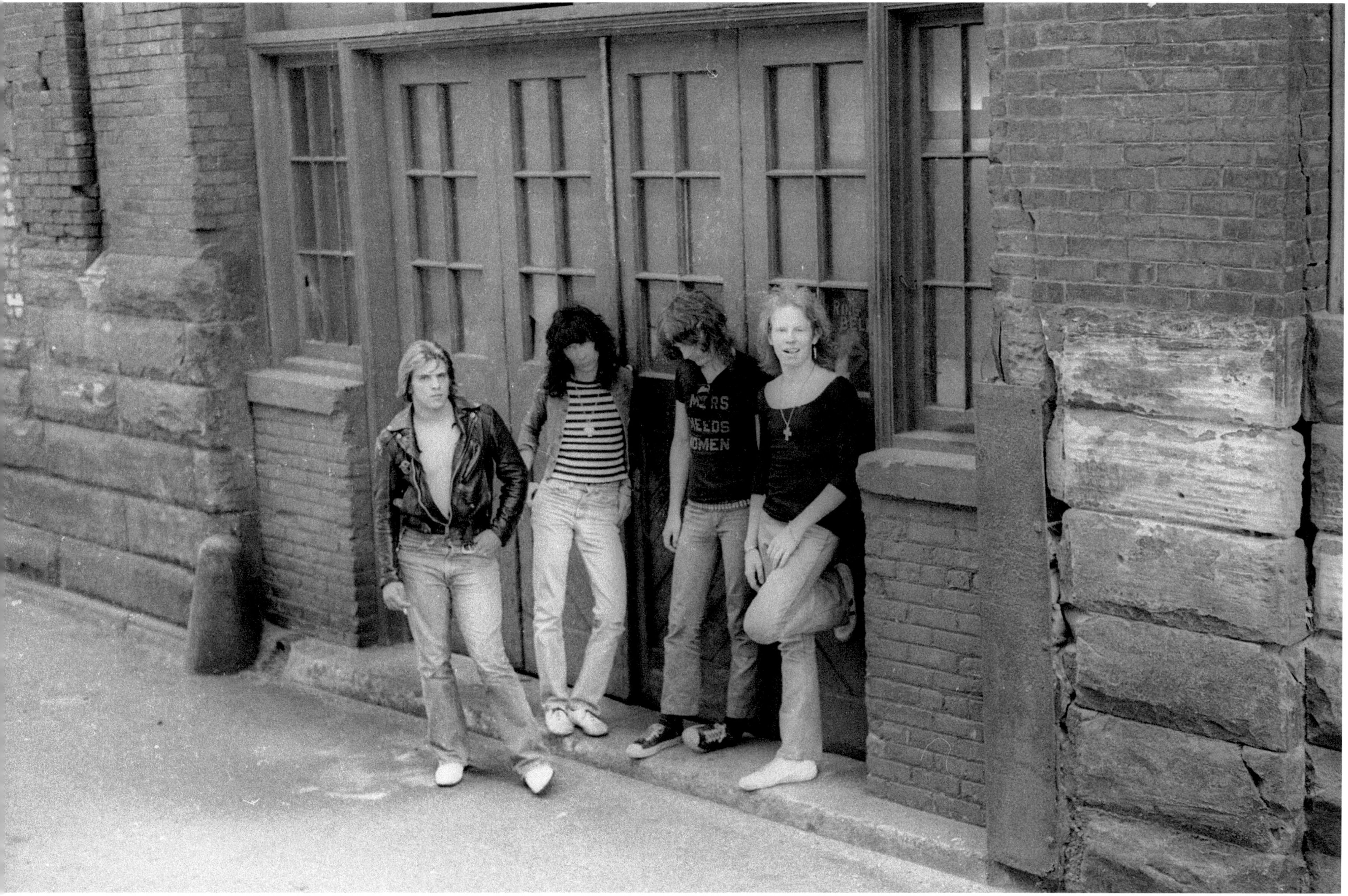

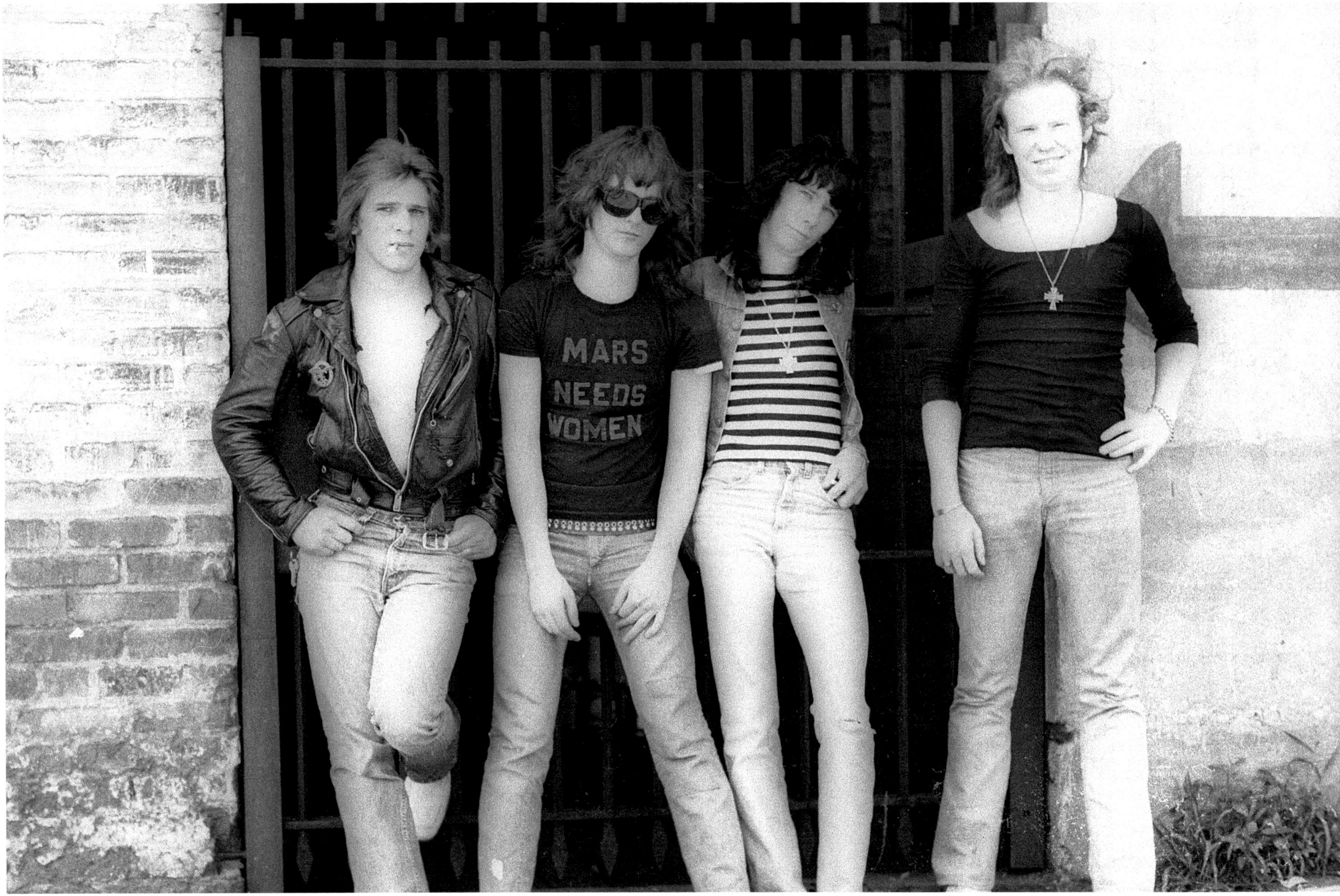
MARS
NEEDS
WOMEN

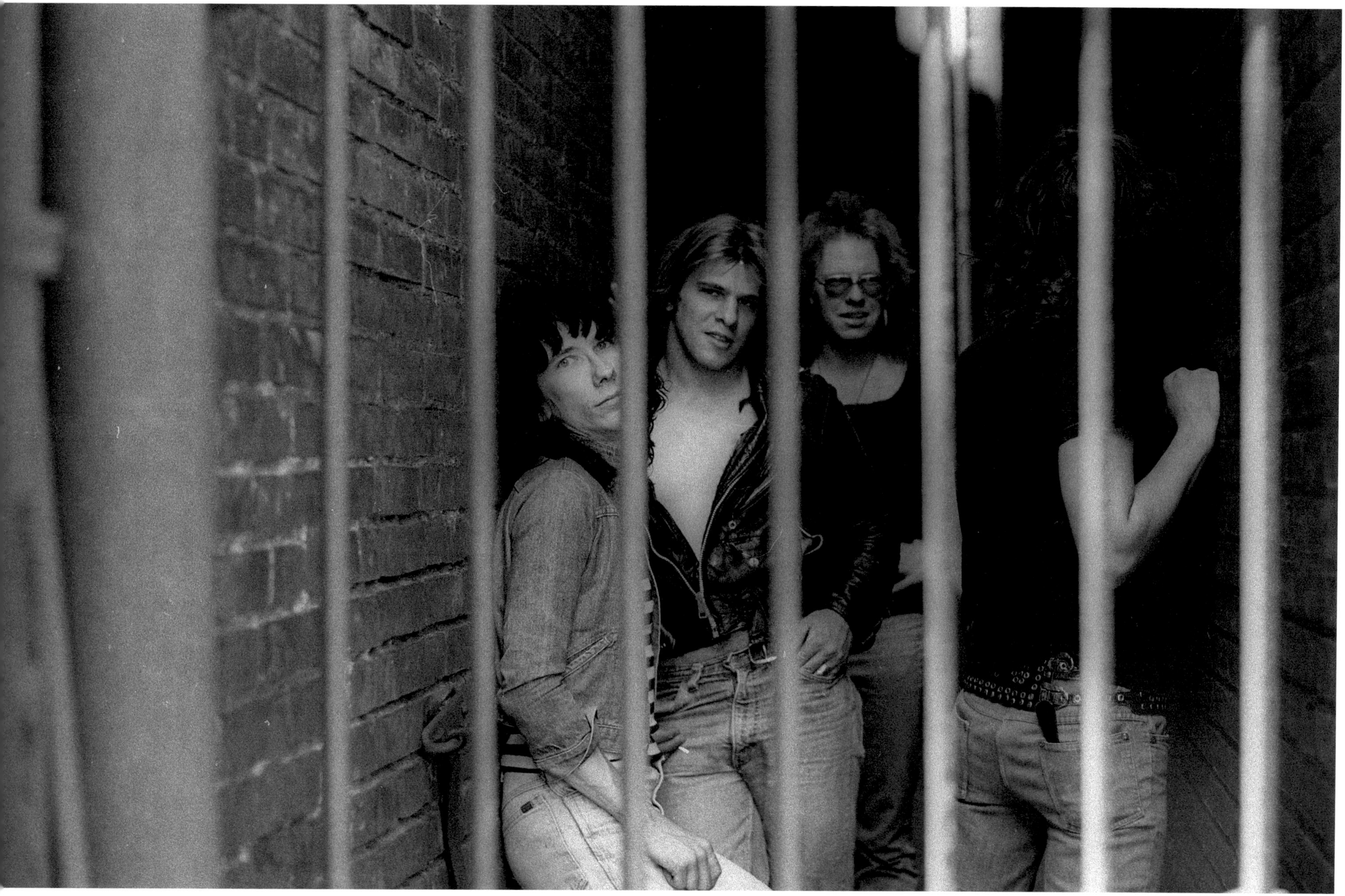

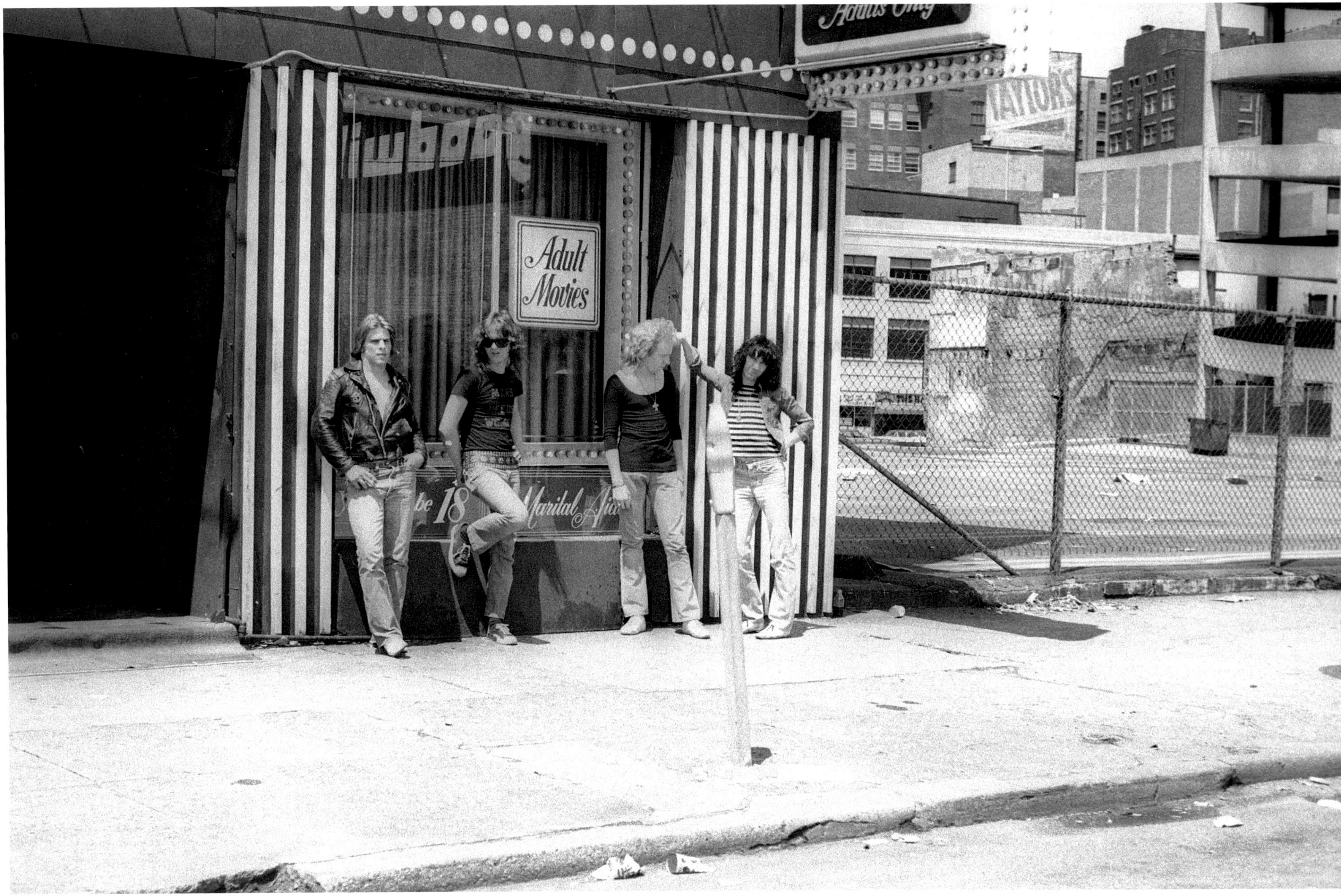
Adults Only
Adult
Movies

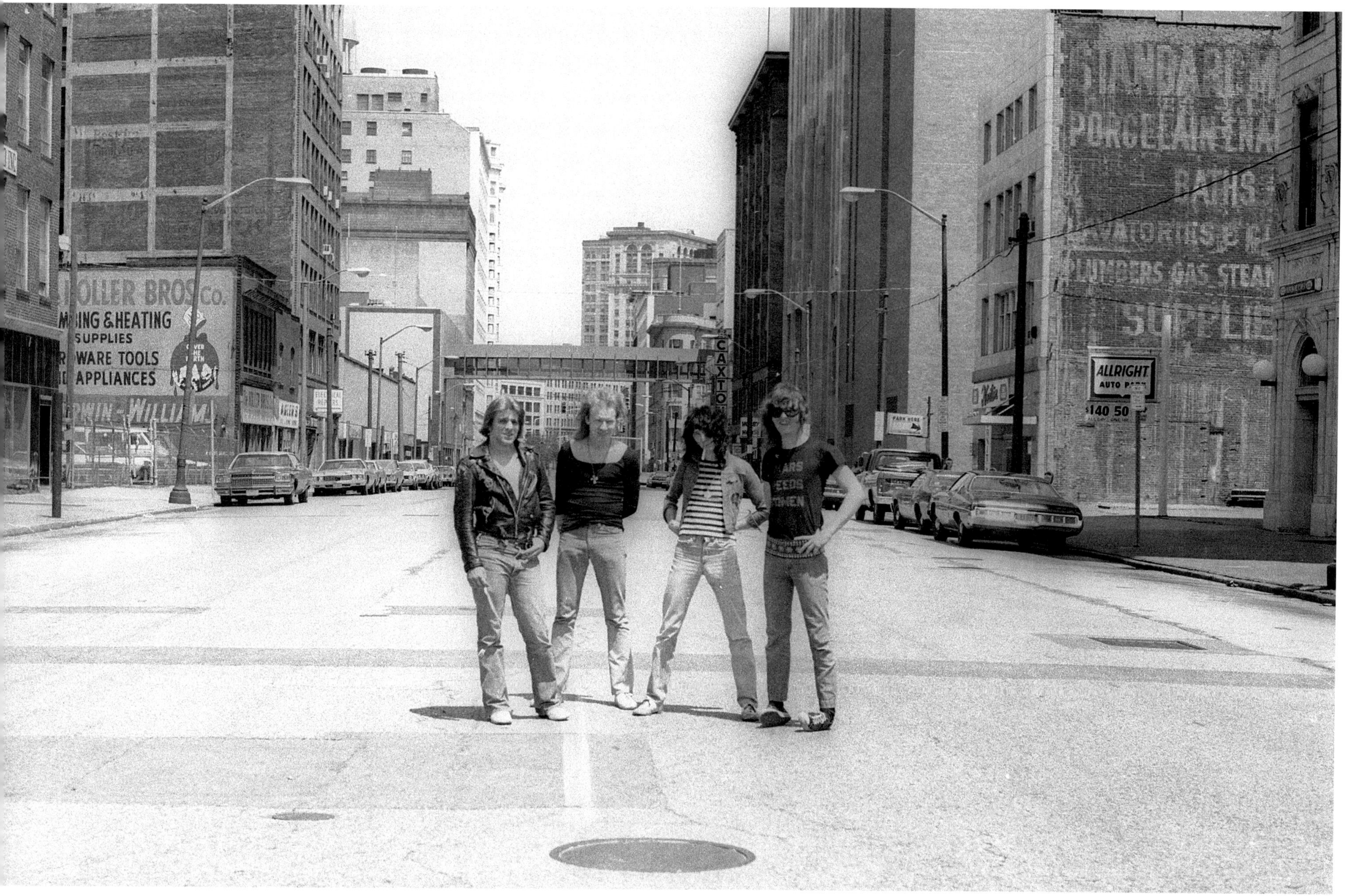
SUPPLIES
APPLIANCES
ALLRIGHT
AUTO PARK
$140 50
PARK HERE
BATHS

Johnny Blitz:

I would expect Jimmy to be doing the mooning, but it's definitely Cheetah showing it all the way. The old "Irish Crack."

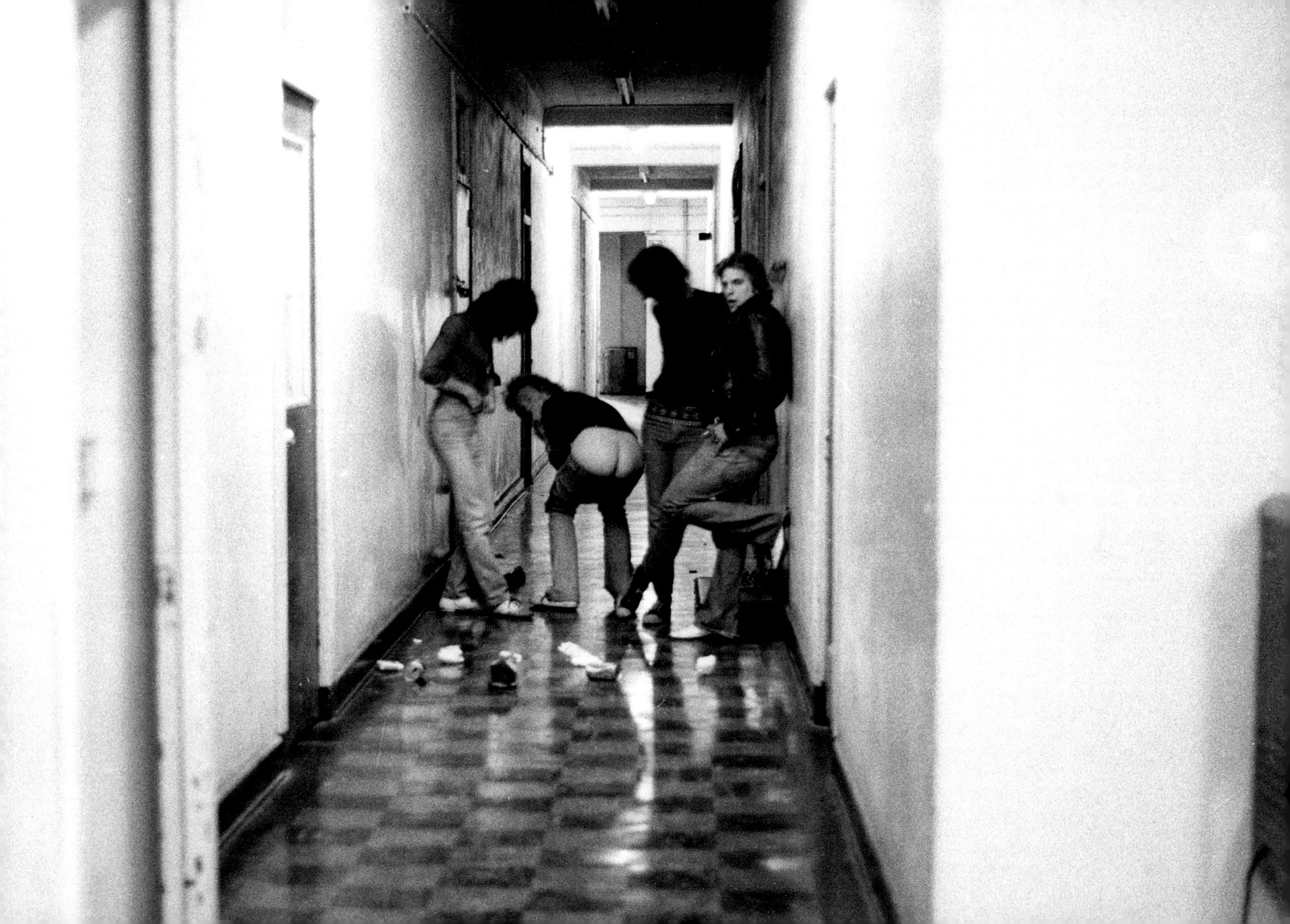

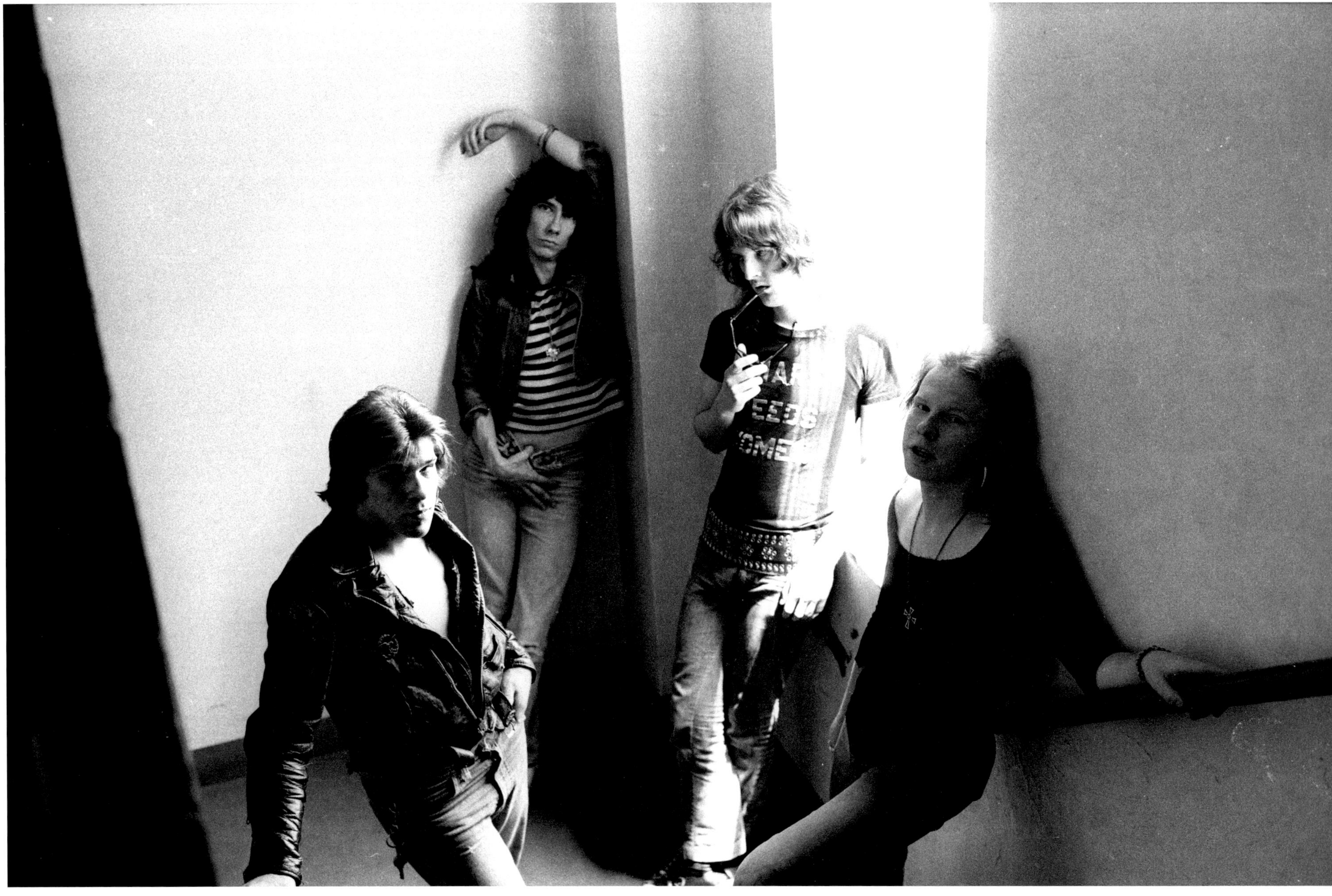

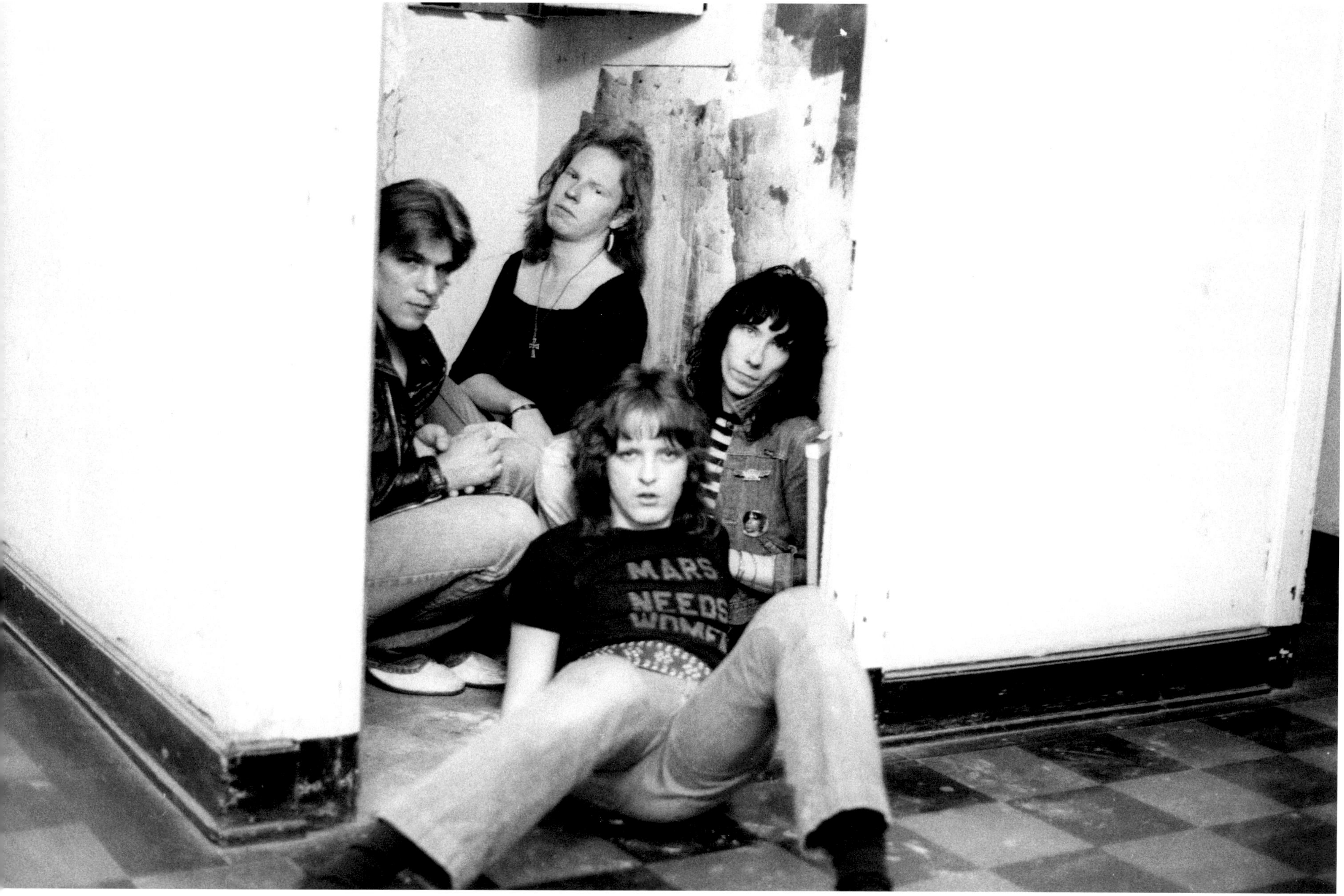
MARS
NEEDS

Cheetah Chrome:

Stiv was in a band called Mother Goose, out of Youngstown. That was the main thing he had going on before us. I met him with Peter Laughner [Rocket/Pere Ubu guitarist, R.I.P. 1977] at the Piccadilly Inn. He kept telling me about Steve Bator, which, you know, was his name—he spelled it "Stiv" but he still pronounced it "Steve," and after it got printed a couple of times everybody started calling him "Stiv," and we said "Oh, shit, now *we* gotta call him 'Stiv.'" We got to be friends real fast, like long lost brothers. There was a short period that he tried to work with Rockets, but that didn't pan out, Stiv was more suited for what we did with the Dead Boys.

Johnny Blitz:

Stiv's personality was so unique. Just a weirdo. Very smart, musically. Natural feel for progression and arrangement. His stage persona was 100% him all the way. What you saw onstage was what you'd probably see if he could be sitting here with us right now. Every night was a new show with Bator, he was such a showman you never knew what he would do, and you looked forward to seeing it.

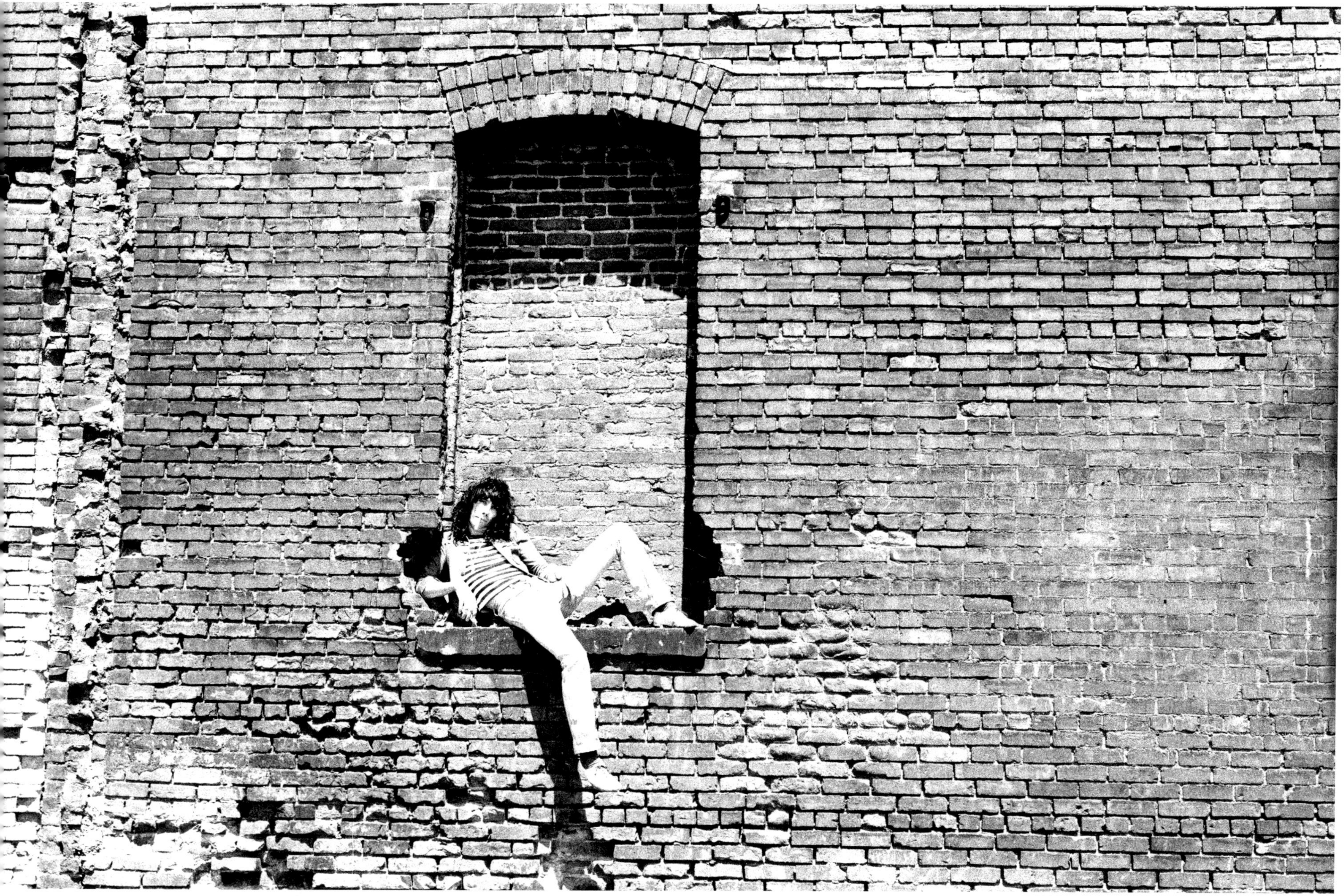

Johnny Blitz:

My father said I was wasting my time playing with Cheetah. My dad HATED him. He couldn't stand him, he'd go "Why are you hanging out with this guy all the time?" I said, "Dad, he's probably one of the most amazing guitarists you'll ever hear in your life," and he'd say, "Oh, bullshit, there's something wrong with that kid." Parents, right? He was just looking out for me, but years later he told me he was wrong about me hanging out with Cheetah. I said, "Yeah, I know you were."

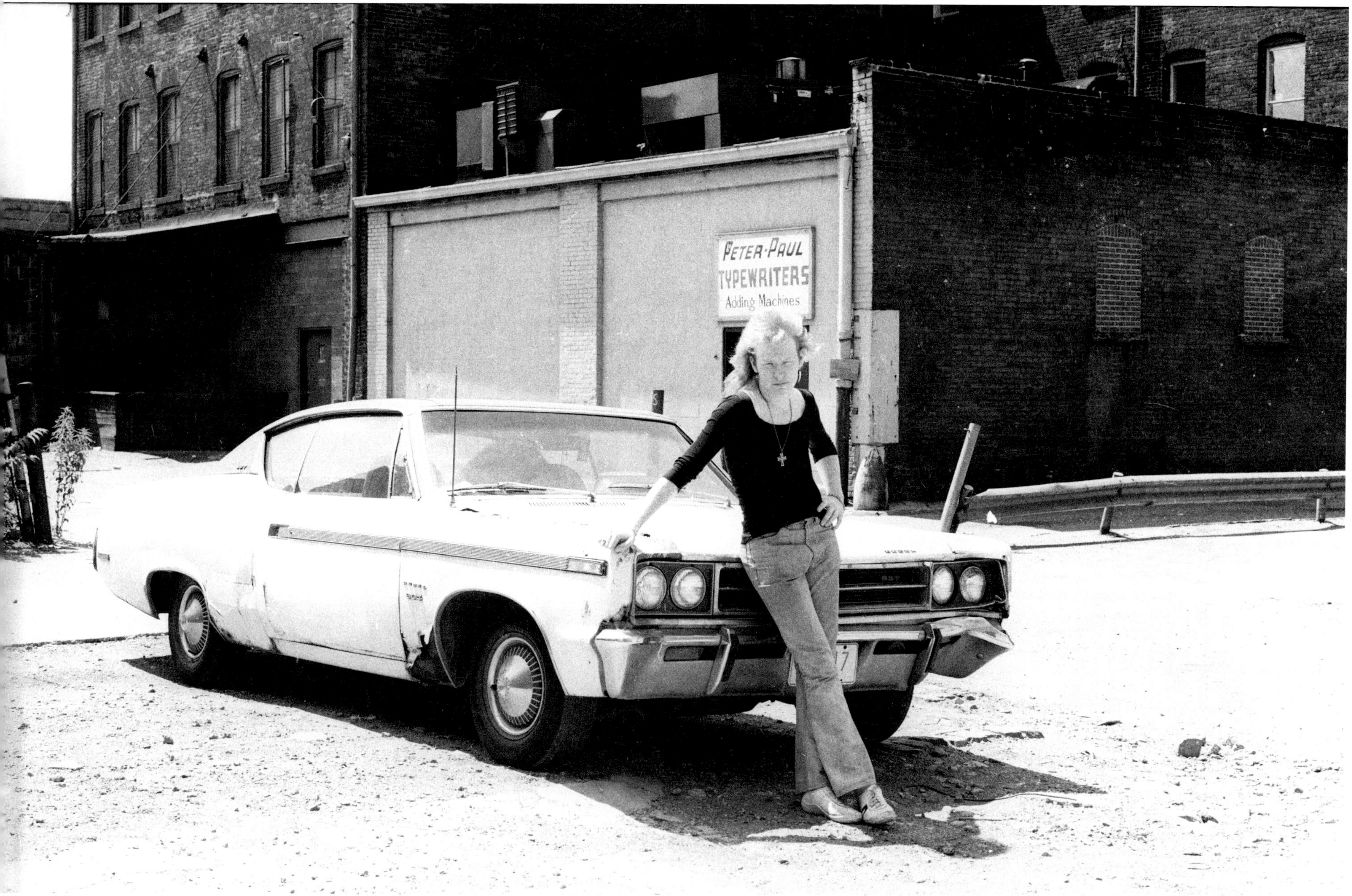
PETER-PAUL
TYPEWRITERS
Adding Machines

Cheetah Chrome:

Johnny and me played together since we were 15 years old. We met through an ad in the paper and started playing in bands in his parents' basement. We did a couple bands that never did anything, but then with Rockets, it started to come together. Blitz quit Rockets fairly early on, he didn't like the situation. I hung around to see Rockets through to its logical conclusion, I was really involved, it meant a lot to me, but as soon as the band broke up I was wanting to get back with Blitz again. We were always hanging out even when he wasn't in the band, anyway.

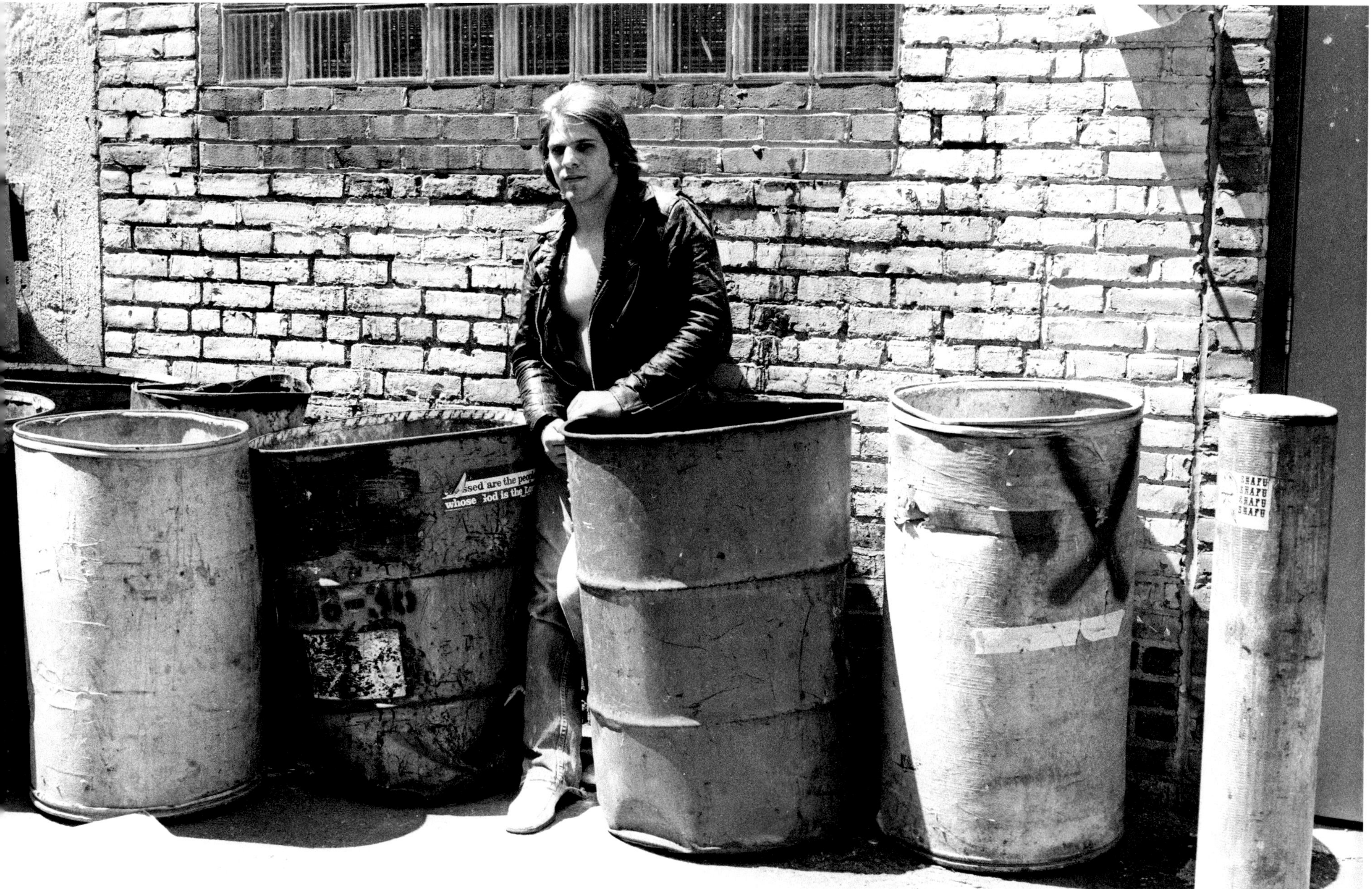
ssed are the peopl
whose God is the Lor
SNAFU
SNAFU
SNAFU
SNAFU

Johnny Blitz:

Jimmy Zero is one of my best friends ever. He's just an amazing guy. He'd never done much before we played with him, he was a bass player, basically. Cheetah called me after I split Rockets—and this was after I expected to never play with him again because he thought I was an asshole for splitting Rockets—but Cheetah calls me and says, "Look, I got these two guys that want to do a band with us, Bator and his buddy Jimmy." I jumped at the opportunity, and it took off.

Cheetah Chrome:

I met Jimmy right after I met Stiv. He was a great guitar player, I've always said he was one of the best rhythm guitar players around, still, to this day, and he wasn't really a slouch on lead either. He had the same sick kind of sense of humor that we shared, same kind of outlook on life, so Jimmy fit right in wth us.

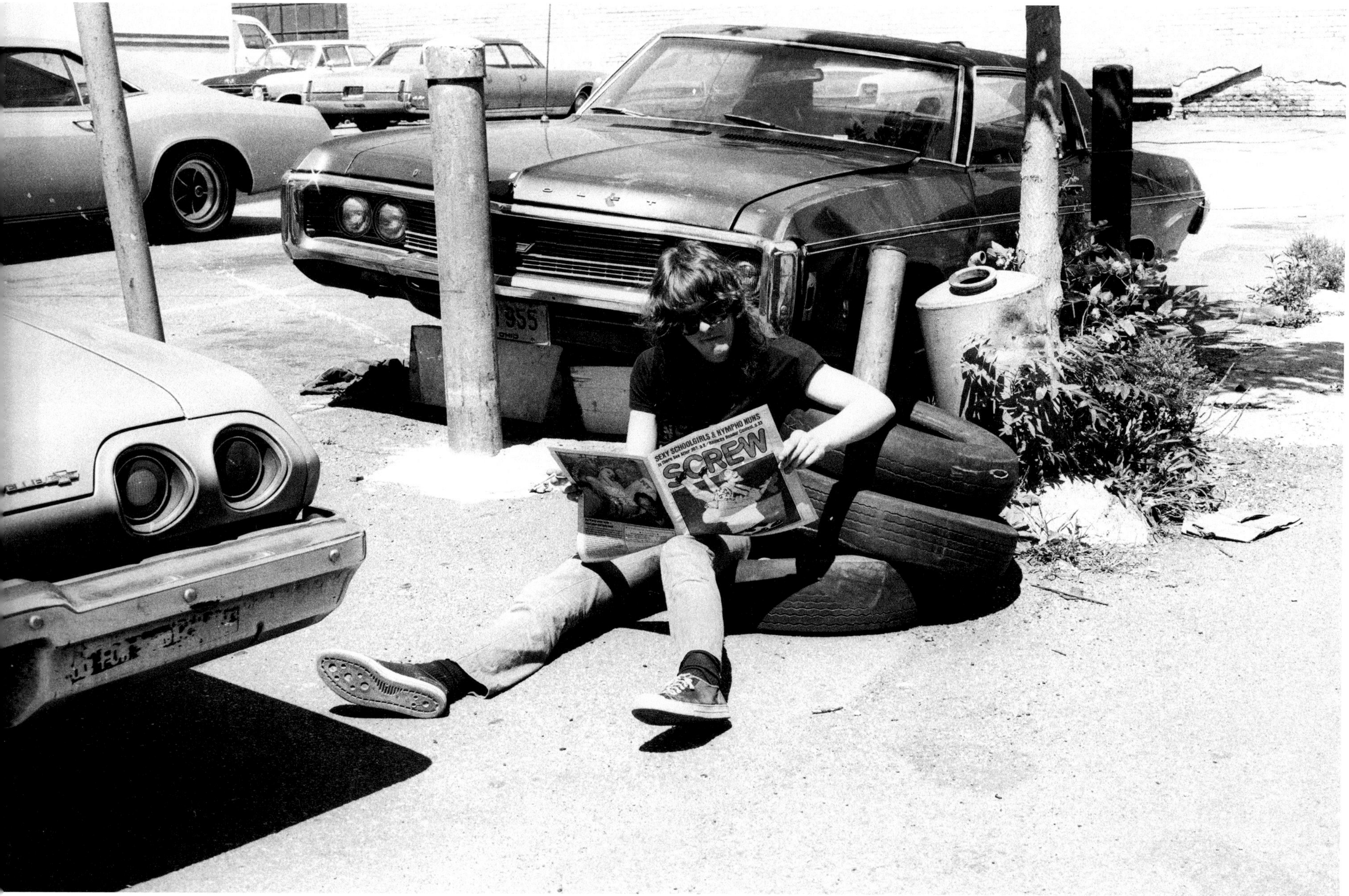
SEXY SCHOOLGIRLS & NYMPHO NUNS
SCREW

PART II: IN CONCERT

THE PHOTOS REPRODUCED HERE HAVE NEVER BEEN SEEN BEFORE this publication, save for a few that were exhibited only once, in Los Angeles in February 2016. They depict two Dead Boys concerts in 1977. The black-and-white shots are from what may have been their last Cleveland performance before they moved to New York. The color images are from a pretty quickly realized homecoming—in July of 1977, they returned to Cleveland to support The Dictators at the Agora. As mentioned in the introduction to this book, the opening band that night was Cheap Trick, who whould soon thereafter go on to achieve massive international fame. Amusingly, a contemporary newspaper article referred to the night's lineup as "three New Wave bands." That show was also the first Cleveland performance of The Dead Boys' new bass player, Jeff Magnum.

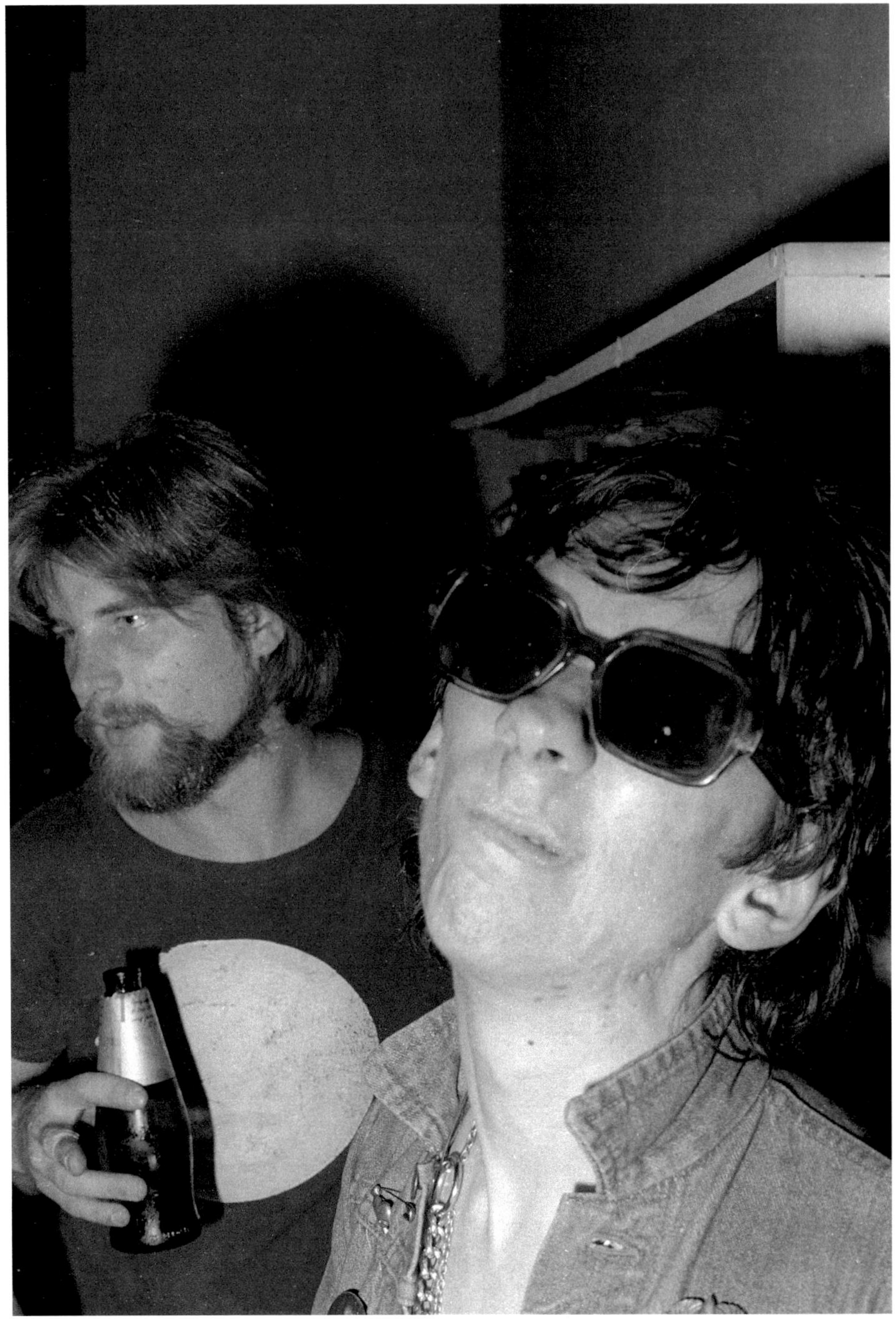

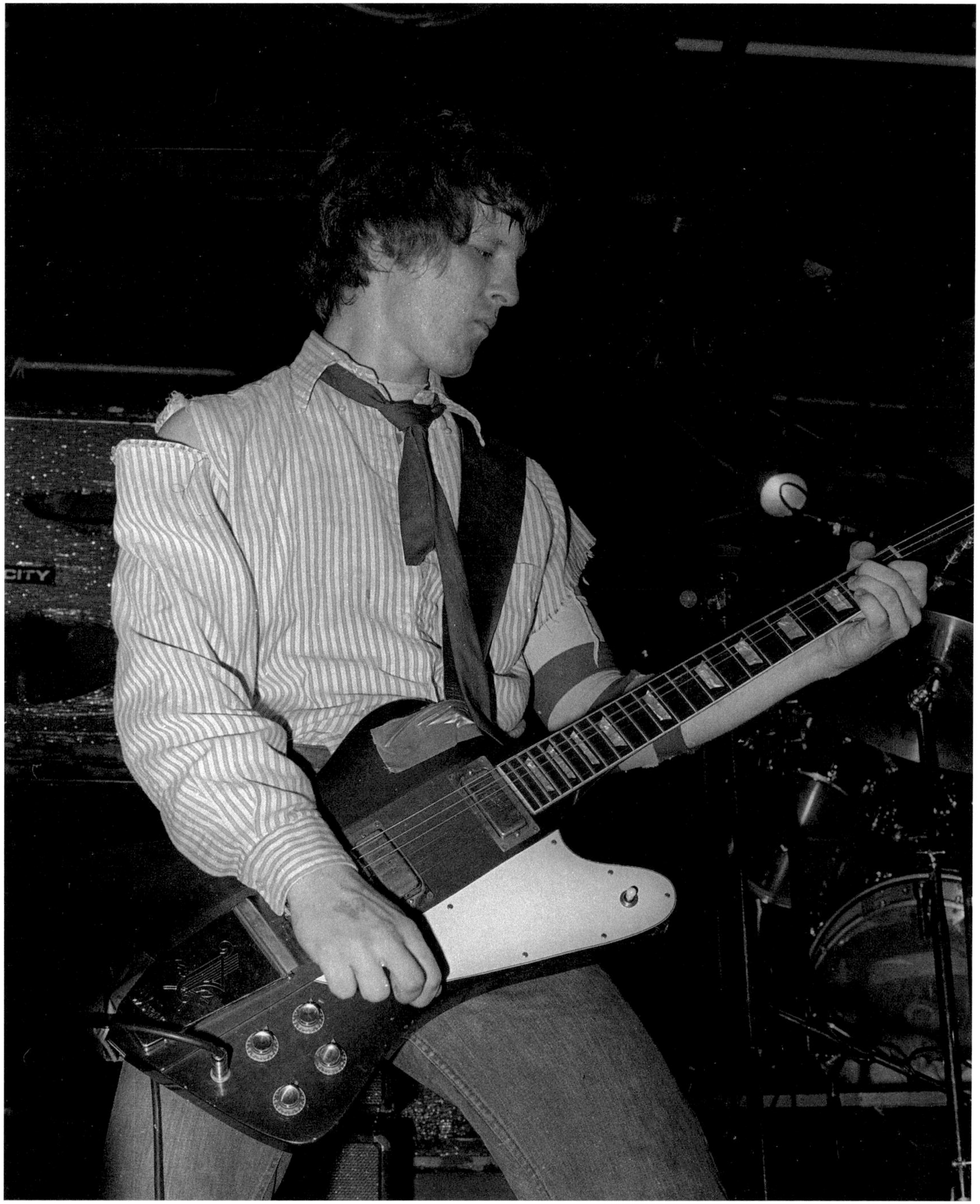

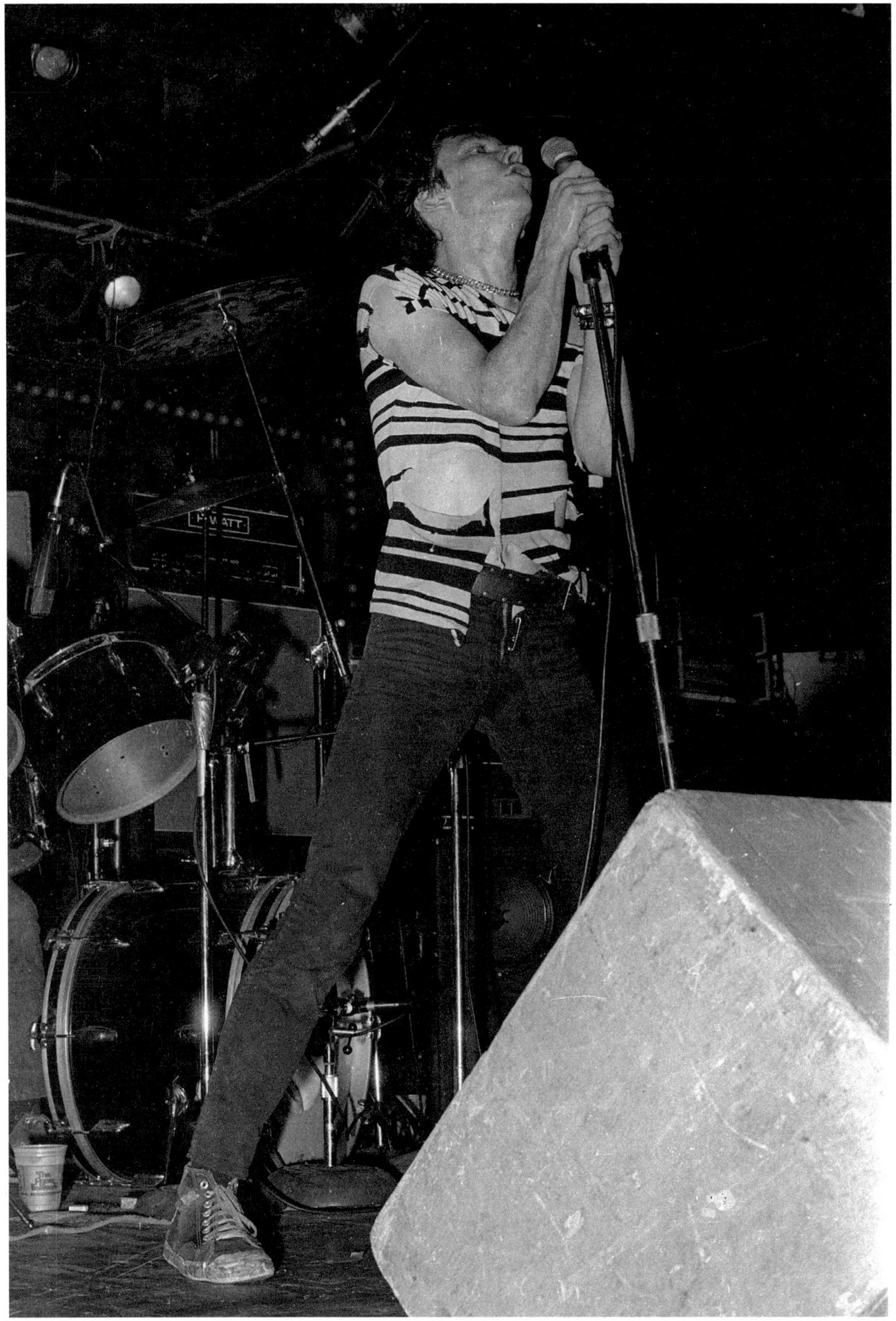

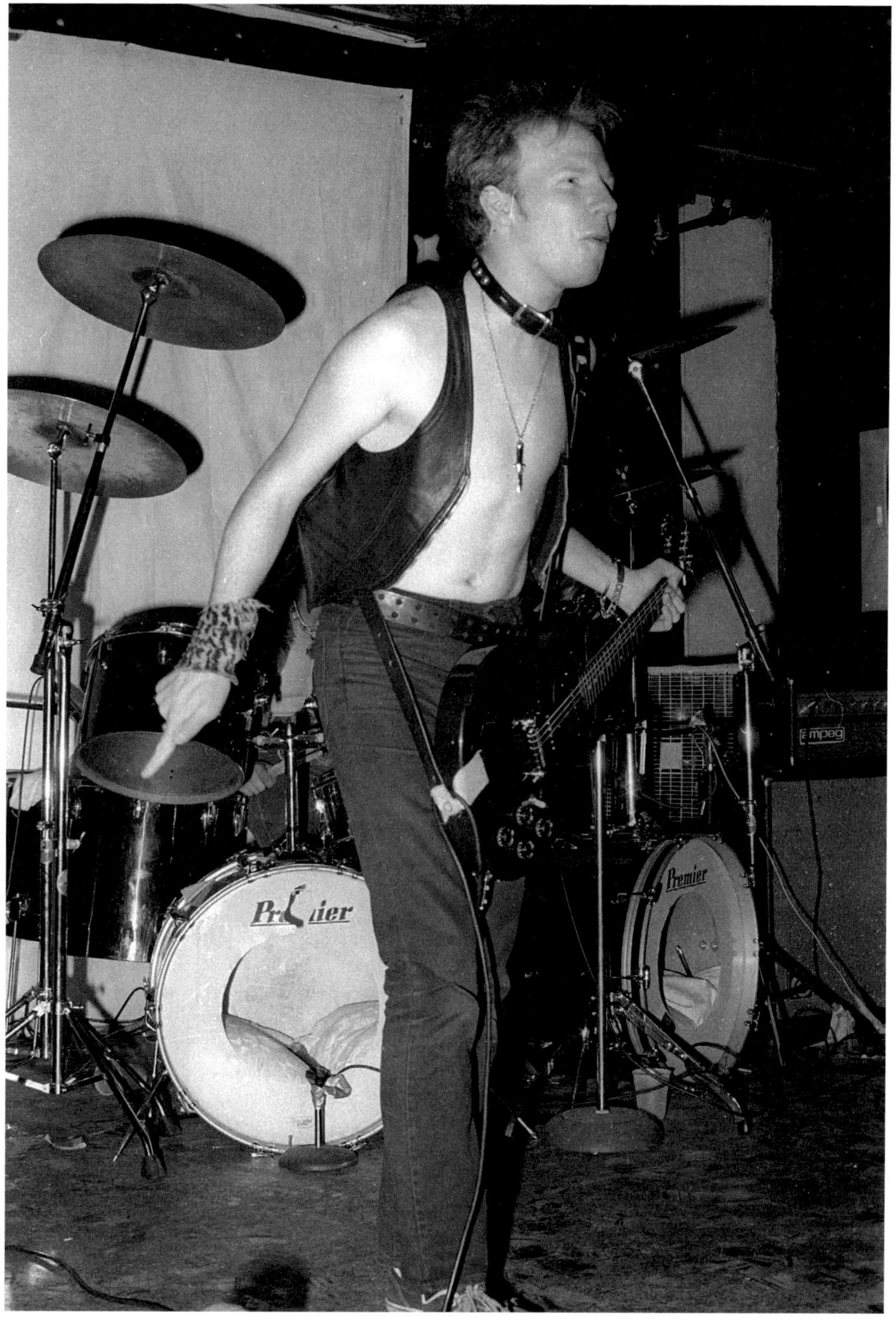
Premier
ampeg

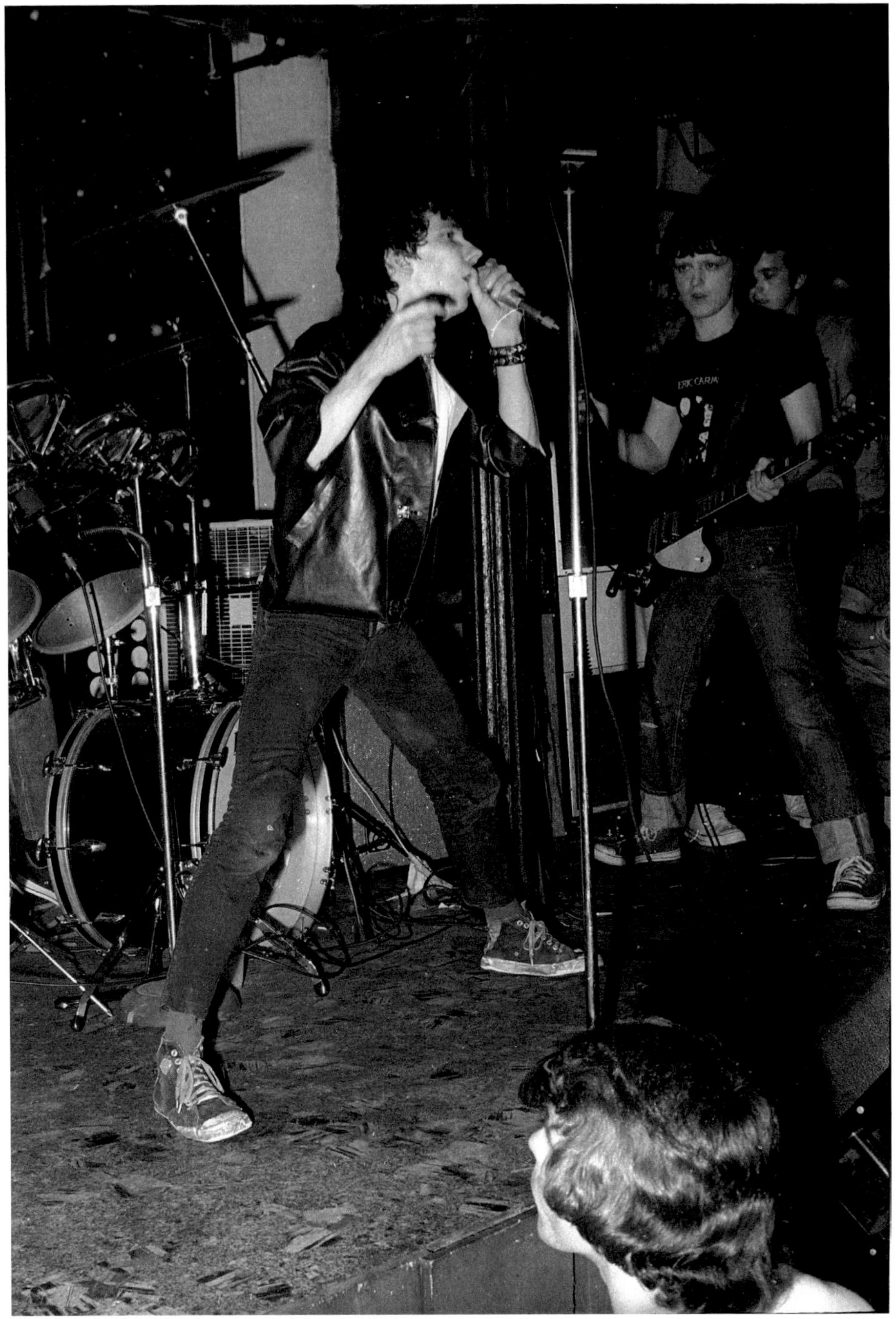

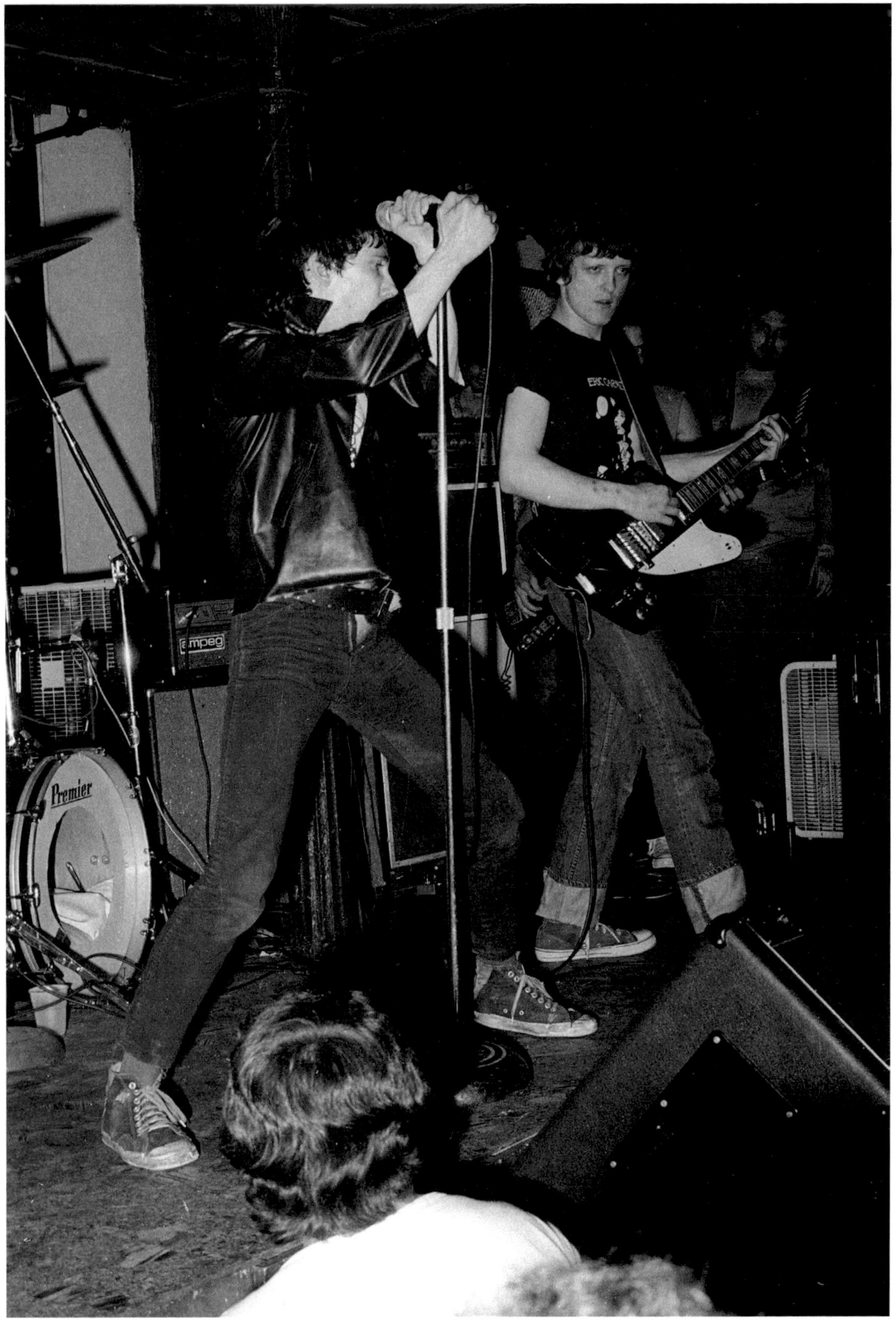
ampeg
Premier

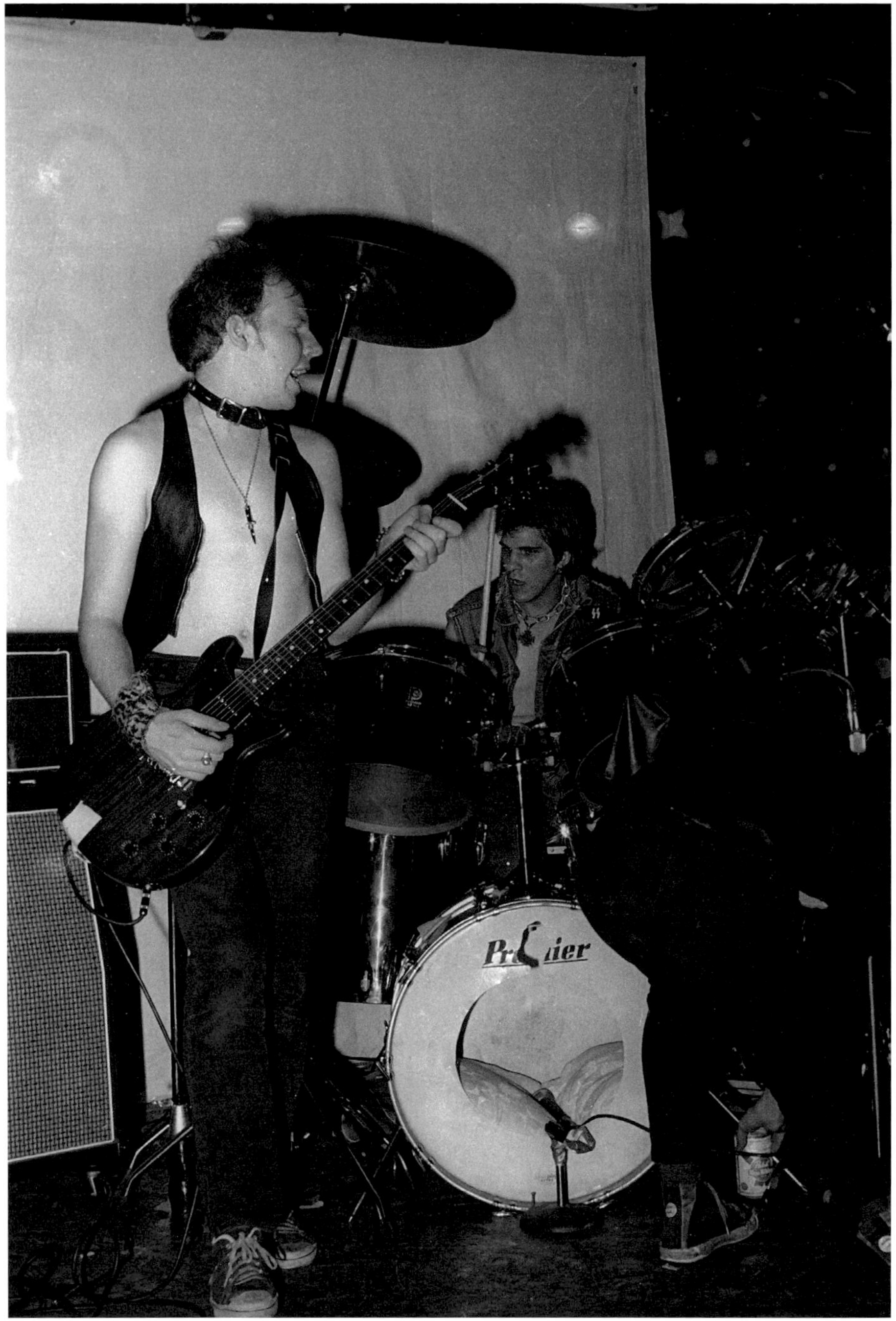

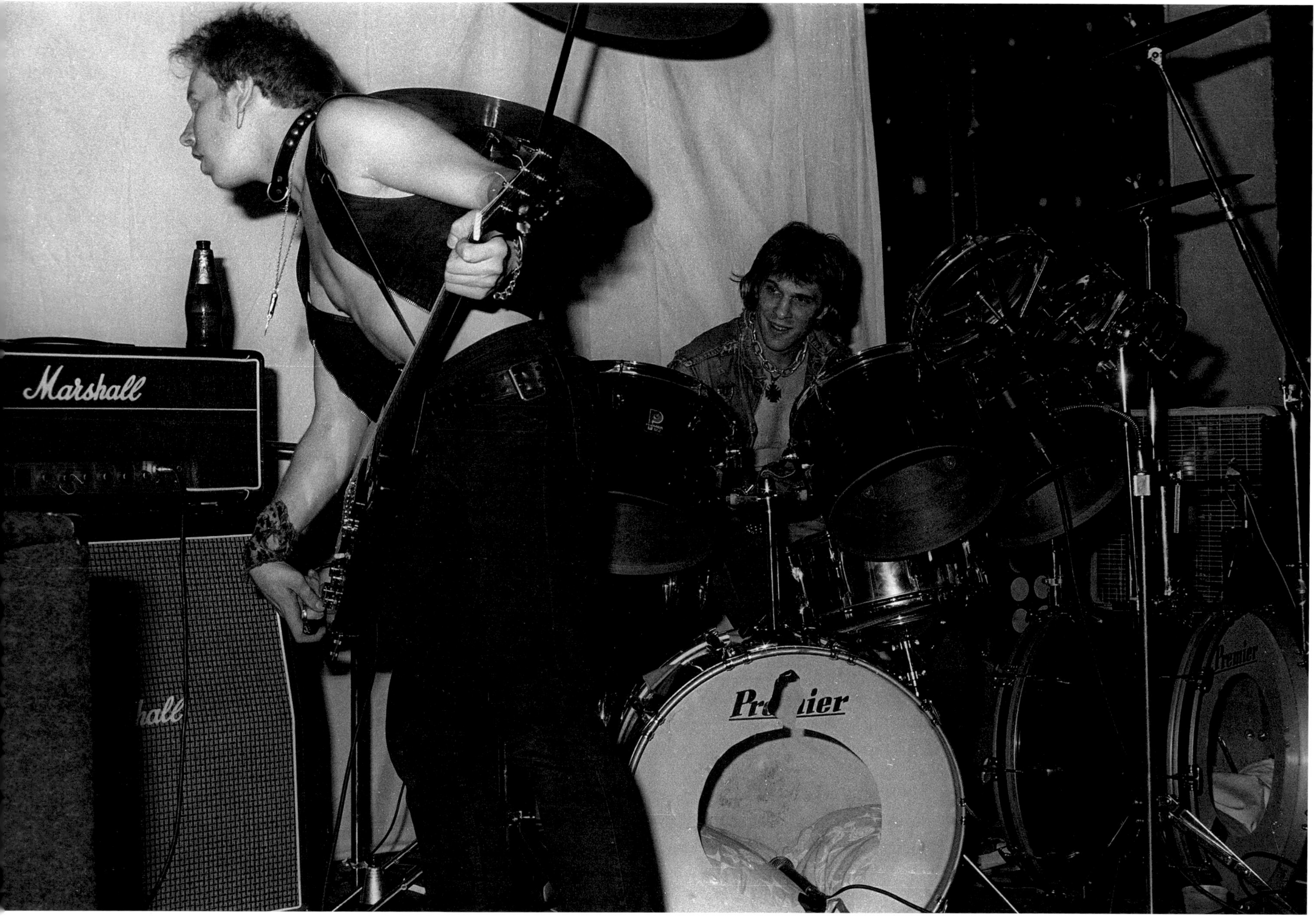
Marshall
Premier

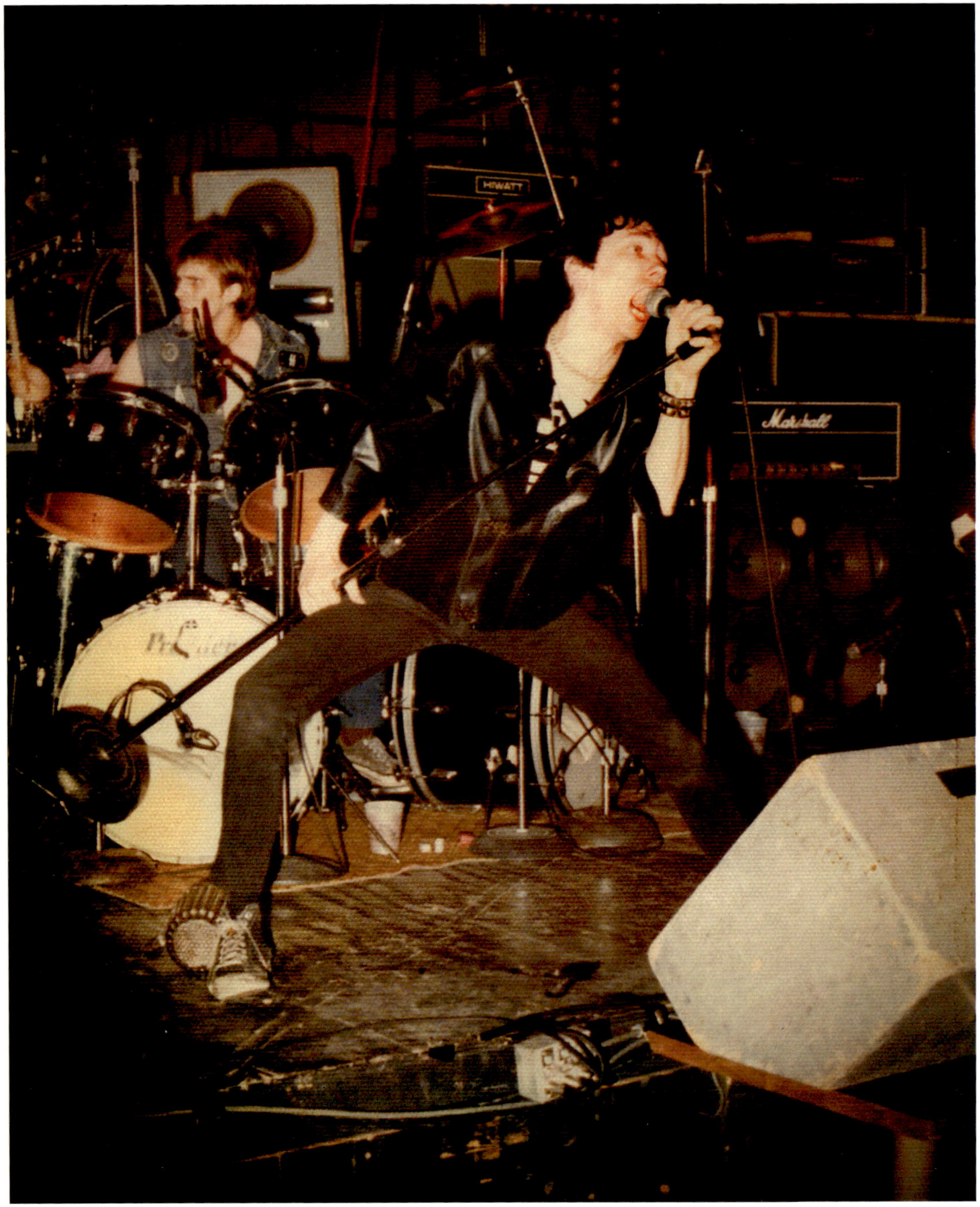
HIWATT
Marshall

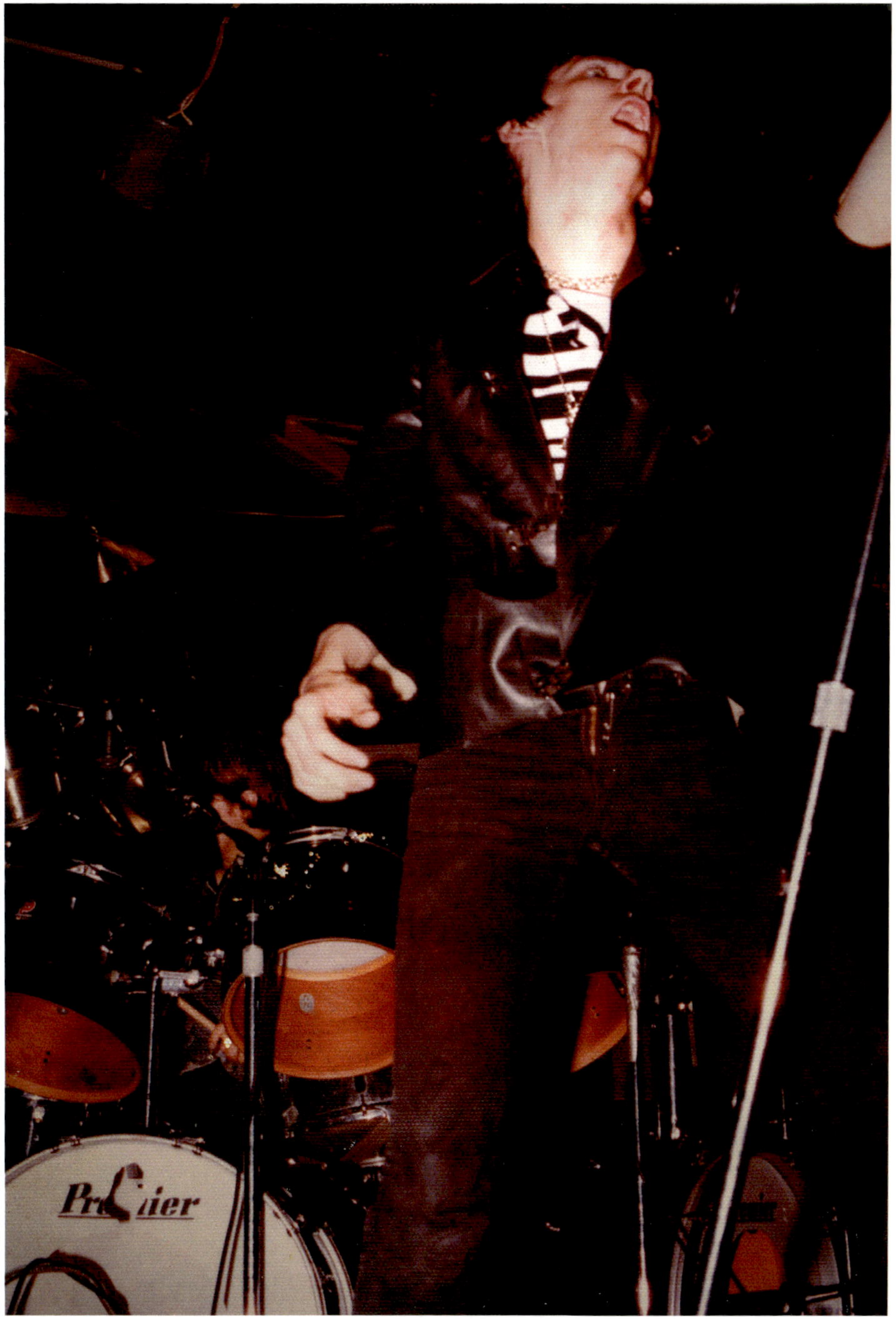

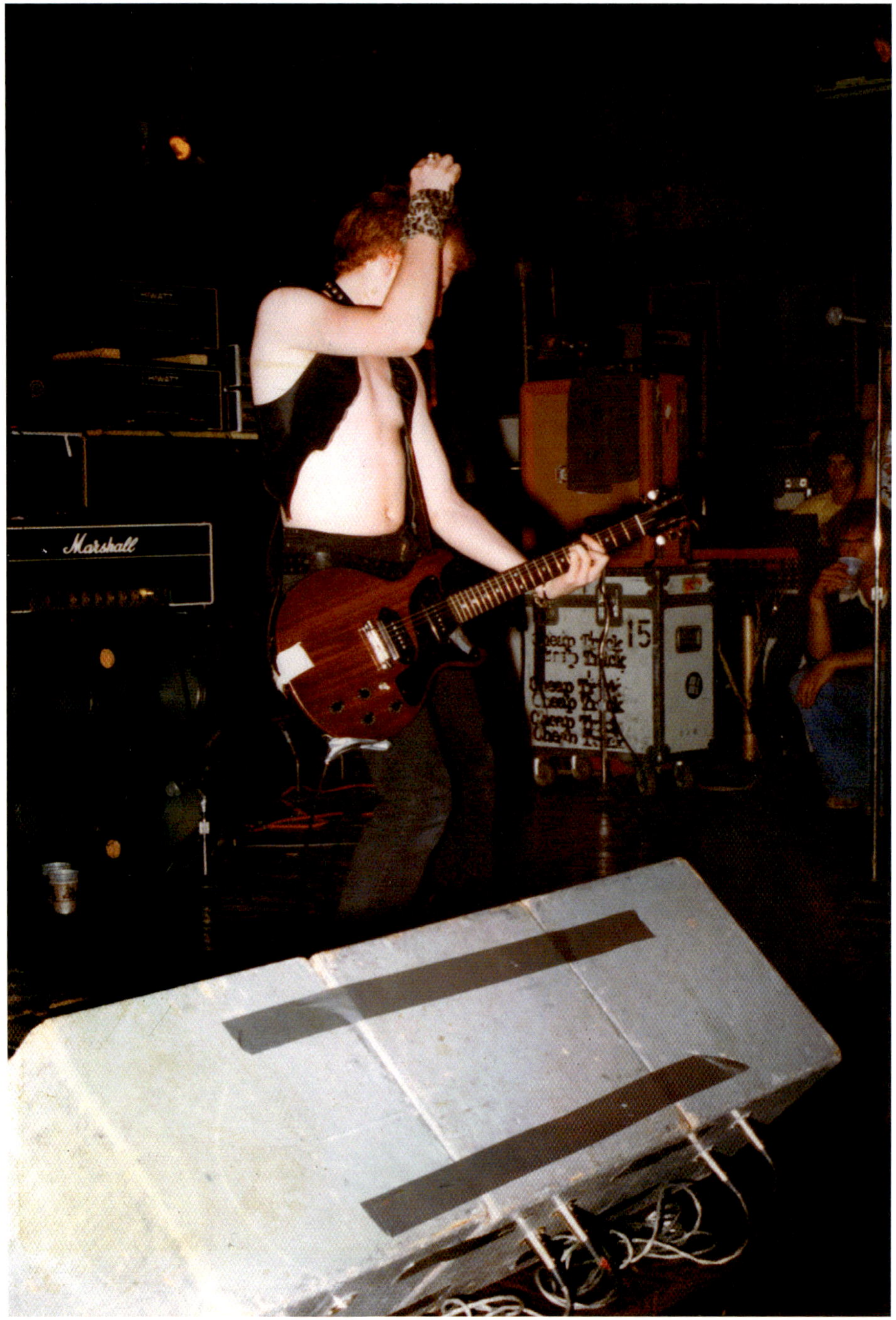
Marshall

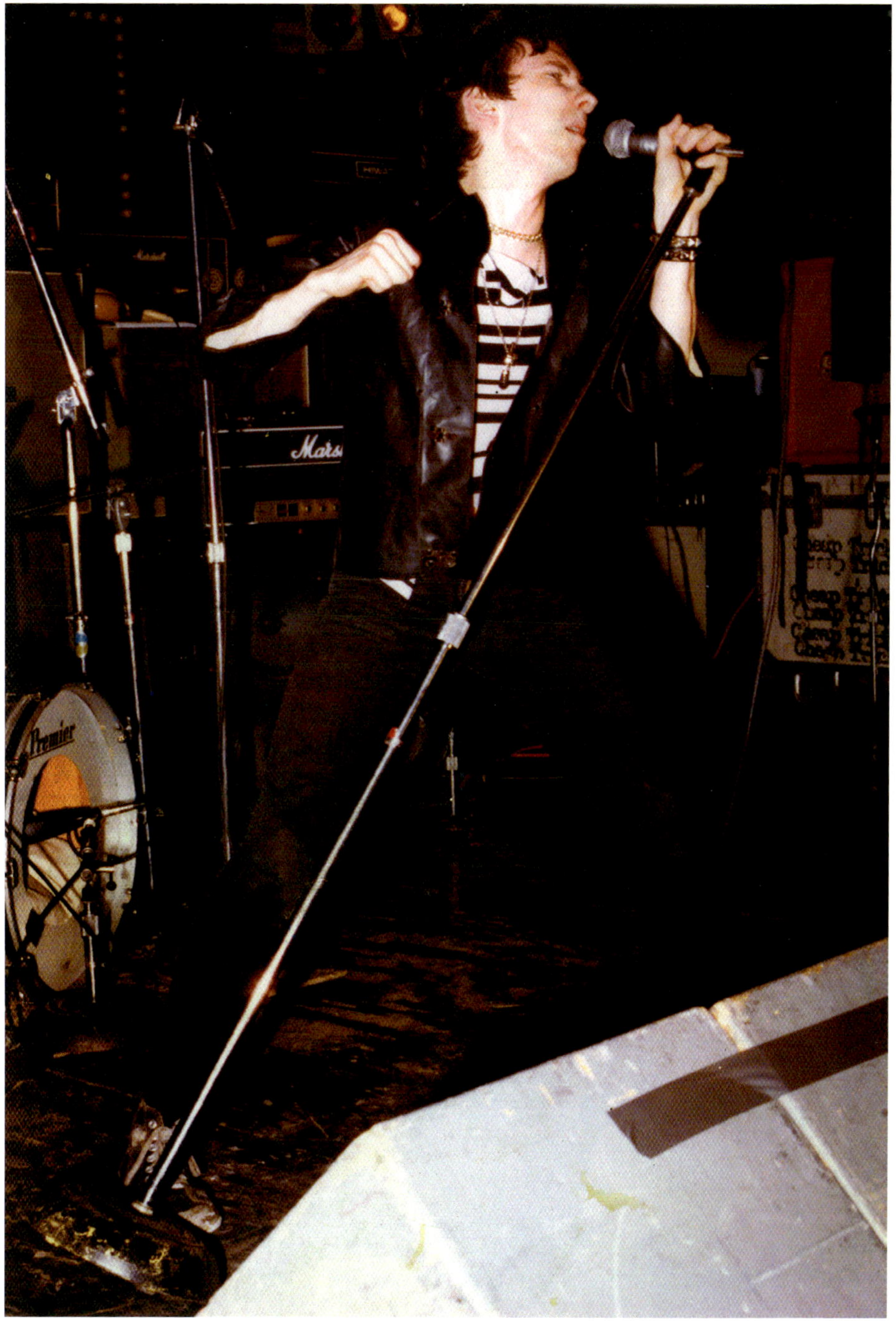
Premier

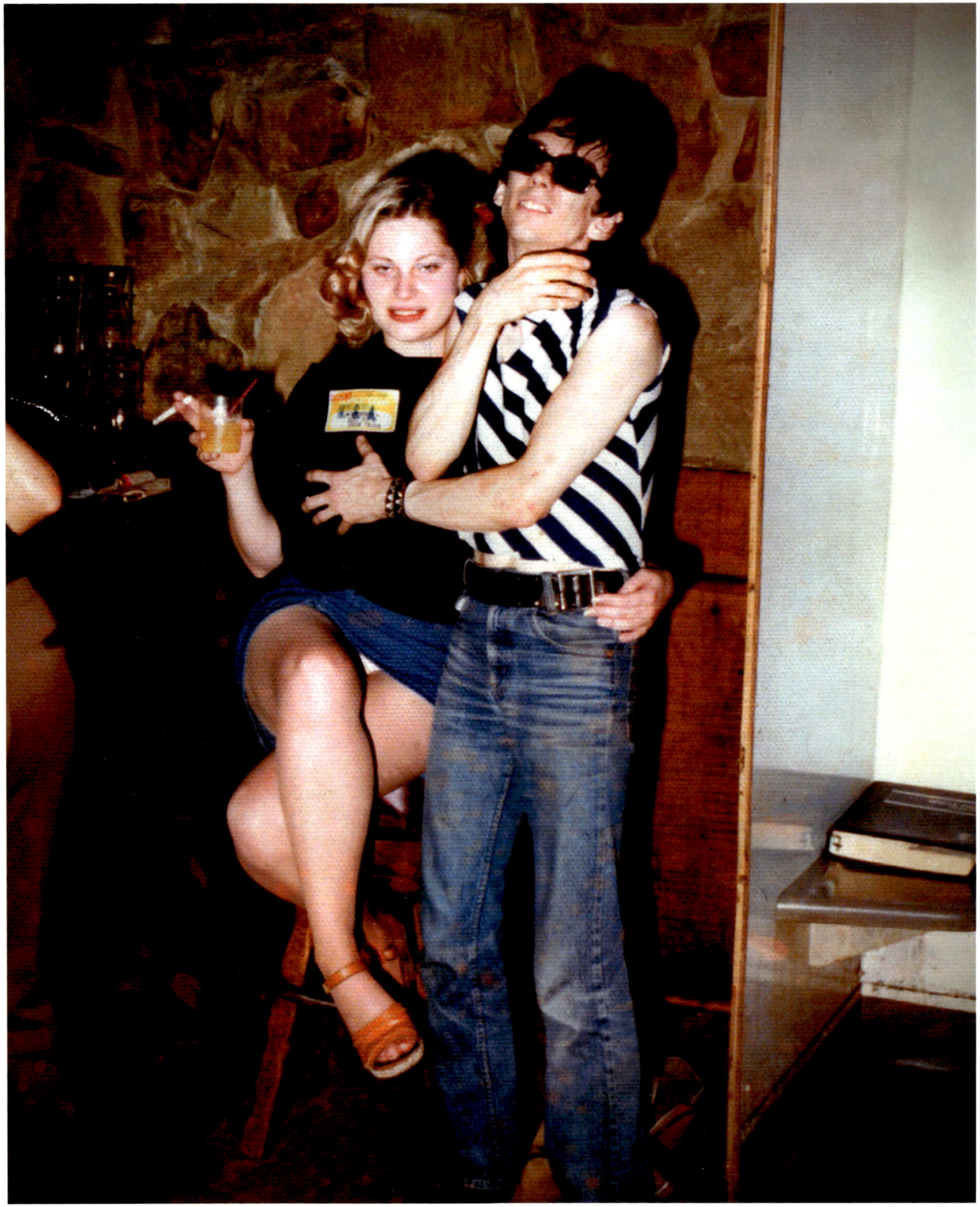

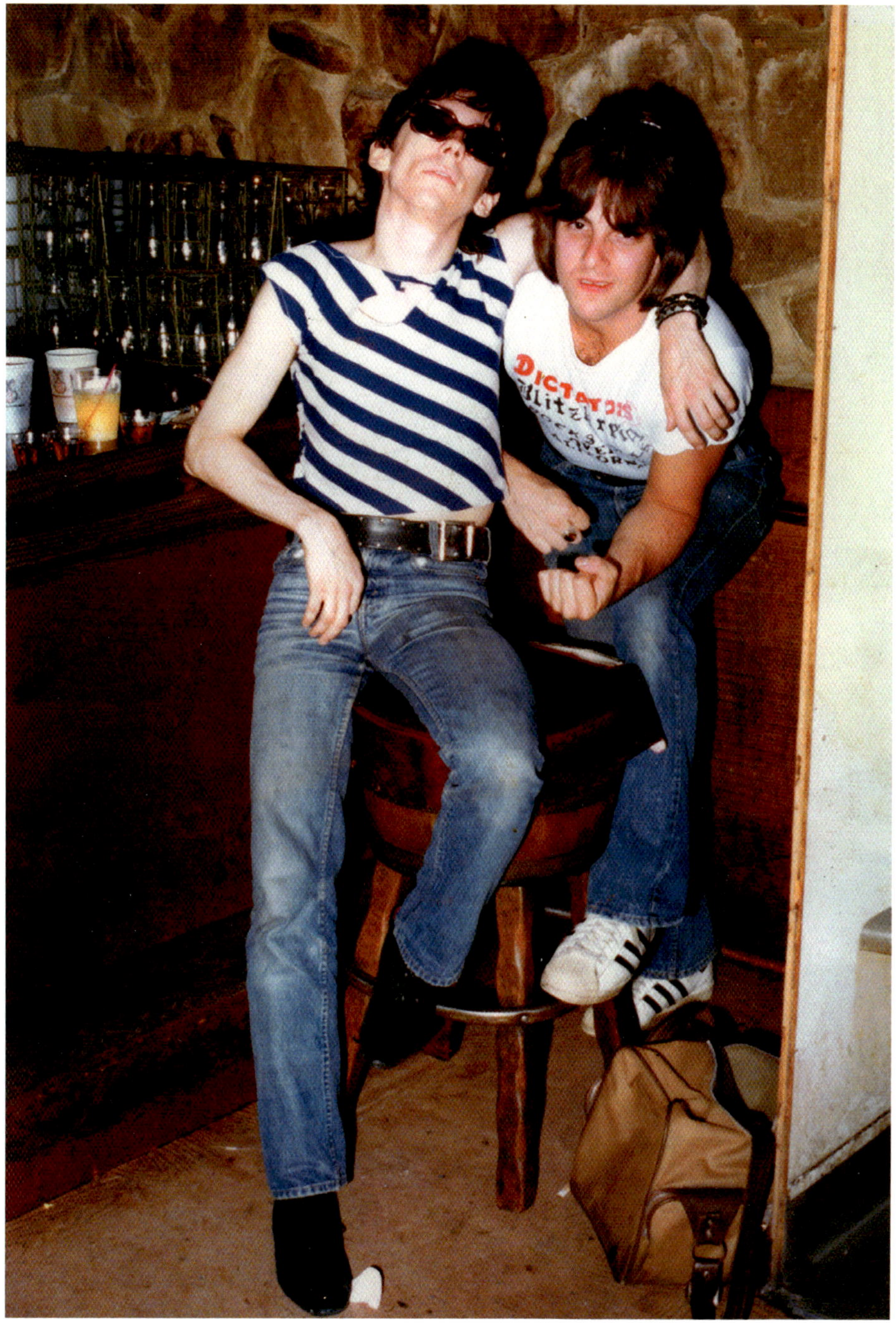

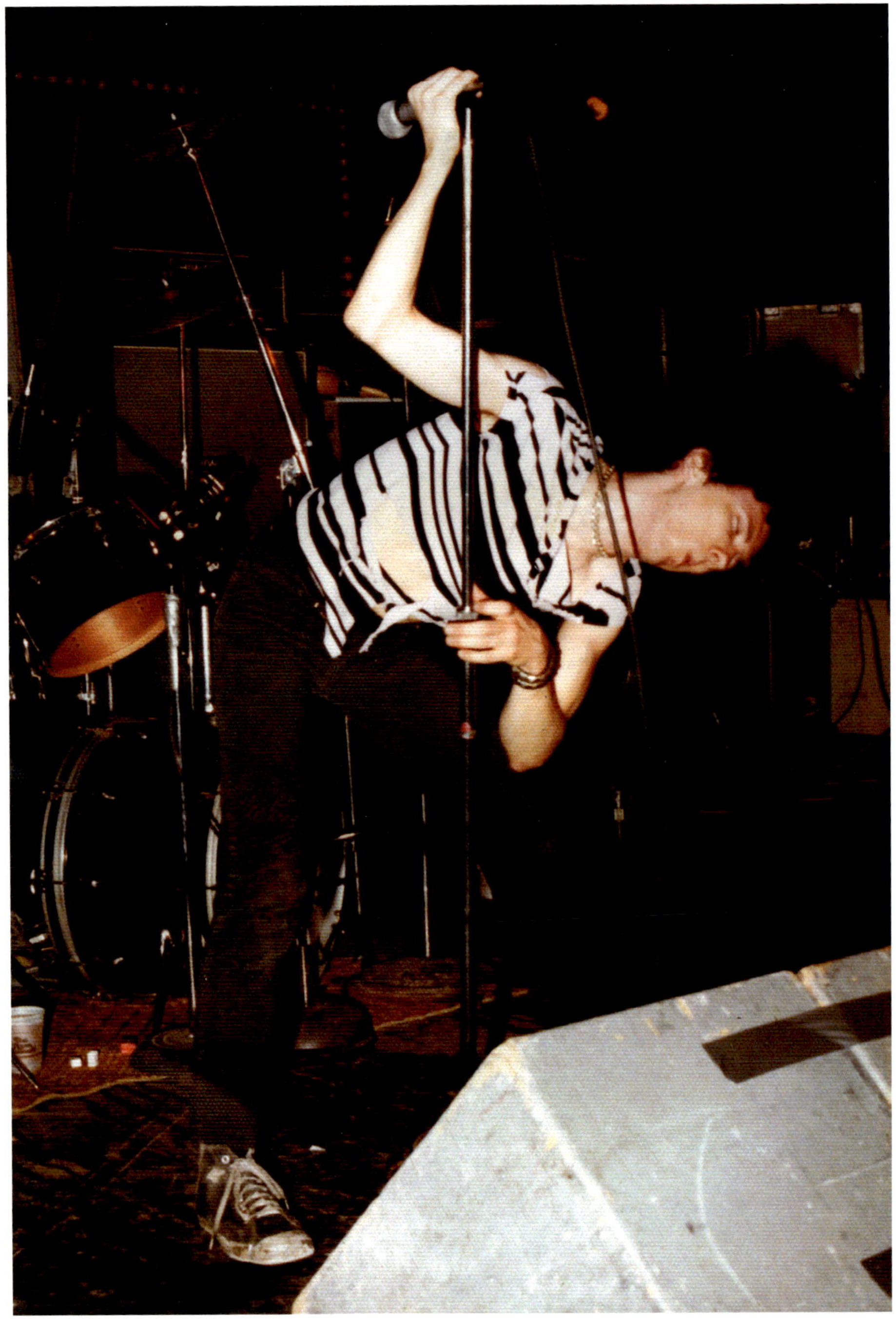

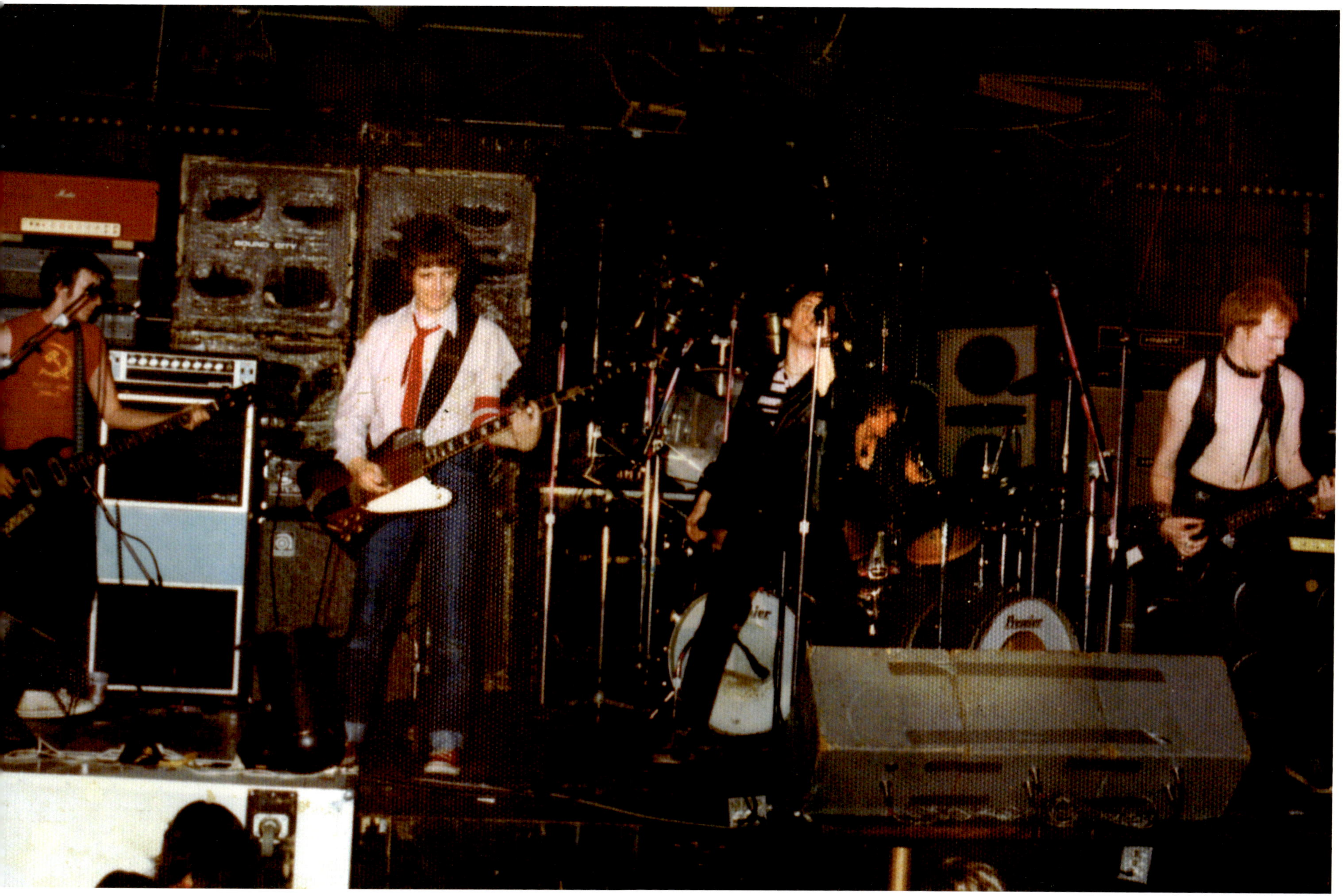
Premier

PART III: STIV BATORS

"ON BECOMING" From *Stiv: 1976, Lost Photographs of Stiv Bators and the Dead Boys*, 2015

IN A NOW INFAMOUS 1970 PERFORMANCE, IGGY POP GYRATED, quaked, and writhed across a Cincinnati stage. Bare-chested and sweaty, he dove into the pulsating crowd and rose triumphantly, in what has now become an iconic image: Iggy standing upright like a general giving the order to charge, supported only by the audience's hands. The star had emerged, oddly enough, with a giant tub of peanut butter—which he then spread all over his naked torso, occasionally scraping up handfuls of the sticky goo to launch into the crowd—all captured for posterity on television. To further add to the legendary nature of this moment, the peanut butter was supposedly given to Iggy by a young man in the audience from Youngstown, Ohio named Steve Bator. The tale may be apocryphal, but if true, this moment carries tremendous weight—unbeknownst to him, Iggy was accepting the prop from a young protégé, a man that was in the process of becoming something different—someone different. Perhaps with this gooey offering to the grandfather of punk, Steve Bator began his transformation into Stiv Bators – and to some extent, these photographs also show us a bit of this "becoming."

The narrative of male performance in rock and roll has a long and storied pedigree, and needn't be beaten to death here. If asked, one could easily build a family tree of rebellious troubadours—from Elvis on *The Ed Sullivan Show* to GG Allin on *The Jerry Springer Show*—peppered with branches for your David Bowies, James Browns, Lux Interiors, Alice Coopers, and Mick Jaggers. Stiv Bators certainly fits somewhere on this "frontman" family tree, artfully perched on a branch of punk. More than a mere vocalist, he too participated in a similar kind of stage posturing, equipped with moves, costumes, props, blood, and a penchant for exposing himself.

But these photographs do not show the onstage, public Stiv—you can visit that guy on YouTube, read about his New York shenanigans in Legs McNeil's *Please Kill Me*, or watch him wield a baseball bat as tough guy "Bo-Bo Belsinger" in John Waters' film *Polyester*. In contrast, these photographs taken by his neighbor Dave Treat in 1976 capture a different Stiv altogether—what they capture is "Stiv" in the making. They offer a rare glimpse into the private life of a young man on the brink of something—with a marked sense of unfettered opportunities and grand plans. There's an unquestionable eagerness in his eyes, a what-do-I-have-to-lose attitude—and even hints of the onstage Stiv being built. He poses quite consciously for the camera, wearing the soon-to-be-comfortable guise of the seductive rock star—lanky, languid, oozing sex appeal and confidence, complete with outrageous platform boots.

But if you look closely you can detect another, more vulnerable side of the performer. Crouched in a corner or staring off into the distance, at times there's a palpable sadness—a peculiar malaise. This too could be a pose—the tortured artist suffering for his art, another frequent component of the rock star myth. But one gets a sense that this side is genuine, and for Stiv rarely seen, which makes these photos all the more special.

In addition to these haunting portraits of Stiv, Treat shot impromptu pictures of Stiv, Cheetah Chrome, Johnny Blitz, and Jimmy for the newly christened band, The Dead Boys. As they wandered around downtown Cleveland that day, you can see they are playing, trying, posing—in some shots they look awkward, in others suave, occasionally tongue-in-cheek, but also serious. This was before they had a bass player, before New York City, before CBGBs, before punk rock fame. Like the solo portraits, in these promo photos I see four young men becoming The Dead Boys—posing the way that rock stars should, full of hope and promise—about to embark on what would be a short-lived yet memorable ride from being the toast of the Village to the depths of drug-addled squalor. Looking at them here, eyes wide and restless, full of energy, they couldn't have known the heavy toll that the rock and roll lifestyle would take on them all. In only three years, The Dead Boys disbanded.

But even briefer was this moment before all that—and that's exactly what makes these photographs so intense. Their gritty texture and fuzziness merely exacerbate that feeling of transience, the spontaneity of it all. But as with all photography, every moment is gone even as it is captured. Time marches on. As Susan Sontag famously pointed out in *On Photography*: "To take a photograph is to participate in another person's mortality, vulnerability, mutability. Precisely by slicing out this moment and freezing it, all photographs testify to time's relentless melt."

In Paris on June 4, 1990, Stiv's time stopped—a life ended far too soon, and so randomly. Fittingly, his ashes were spread across the grave of fellow unruly frontman Jim Morrison. I like to imagine the two of them, brothers in arms, causing trouble in the next life. I just hope they can keep 'em in their pants.

—Brittany M. Hudak, June 4, 2015, Cleveland, Ohio

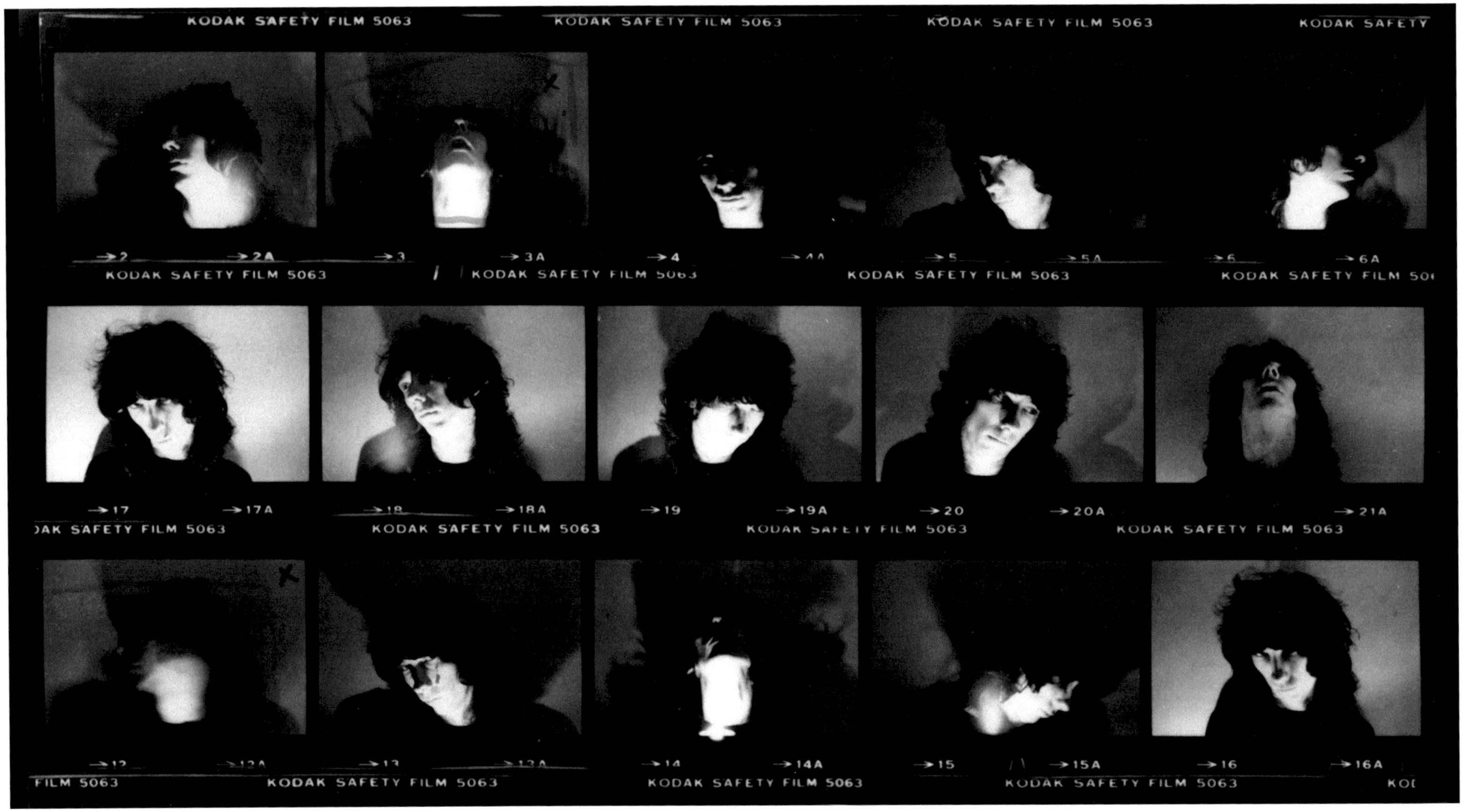
KODAK SAFETY FILM 5063
KODAK SAFETY FILM 5063
KODAK SAFETY FILM 5063
KODAK SAFETY
→2
→2A
→3
→3A
→4
→5
→6
→6A
KODAK SAFETY FILM 5063
KODAK SAFETY FILM 5063
→17
→17A
→18A
→19
→19A
→20
→20A
→21A
KODAK SAFETY FILM 5063
KODAK SAFETY FILM 5063
→14
→14A
→15
→15A
→16
→16A
FILM 5063
KODAK SAFETY FILM 5063
KODAK SAFETY FILM 5063
KODAK SAFETY FILM 5063

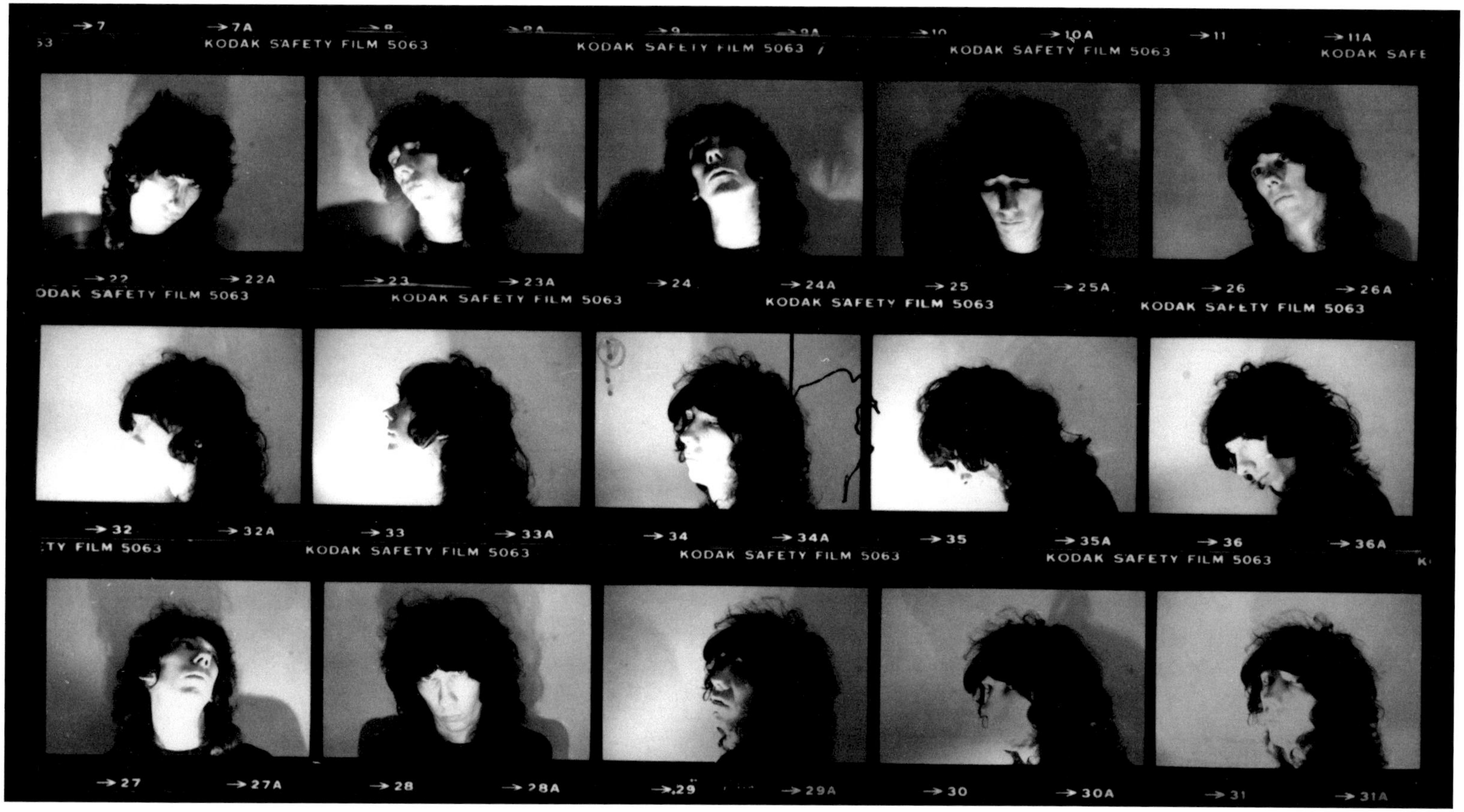
→7 →7A KODAK SAFETY FILM 5063 →10A →11 →11A KODAK SAFE
KODAK SAFETY FILM 5063
KODAK SAFETY FILM 5063
→22 →22A →23 →23A →24 →24A →25 →25A →26 →26A
KODAK SAFETY FILM 5063
KODAK SAFETY FILM 5063
KODAK SAFETY FILM 5063
KODAK SAFETY FILM 5063
→32 →32A →33 →33A →34 →34A →35 →35A →36 →36A
KODAK SAFETY FILM 5063
KODAK SAFETY FILM 5063
KODAK SAFETY FILM 5063
→27 →27A →28 →28A →29 →29A →30 →30A →31 →31A

Johnny Blitz:

We used to call Stiv the "Evil Weasel" because he was a little conniver. He'd have made a great used car salesman. He could sell you on anything he thought you'd want to hear. I truly believe that without him we'd have never gone anywhere. Just the fact of his salesmanship. He sold [CBGB owner] Hilly Kristal, he sold Warner Brothers. He was a freak of nature. The ways he could contort himself—I used to play double bass drums, and he would crawl through my legs and between the bass drums while I played without even touching me, like a little reptile!

Cheetah Chrome:

Stiv was always up to something. There was no "normal" time around him. A normal day, he was up to something at all times, but to me that was the fun! Most of the time we were working on music and having beers, sitting around hanging. I think Jimmy came up with calling him "Evil Weasel," after a Warner Brothers cartoon, because he was always plotting something.

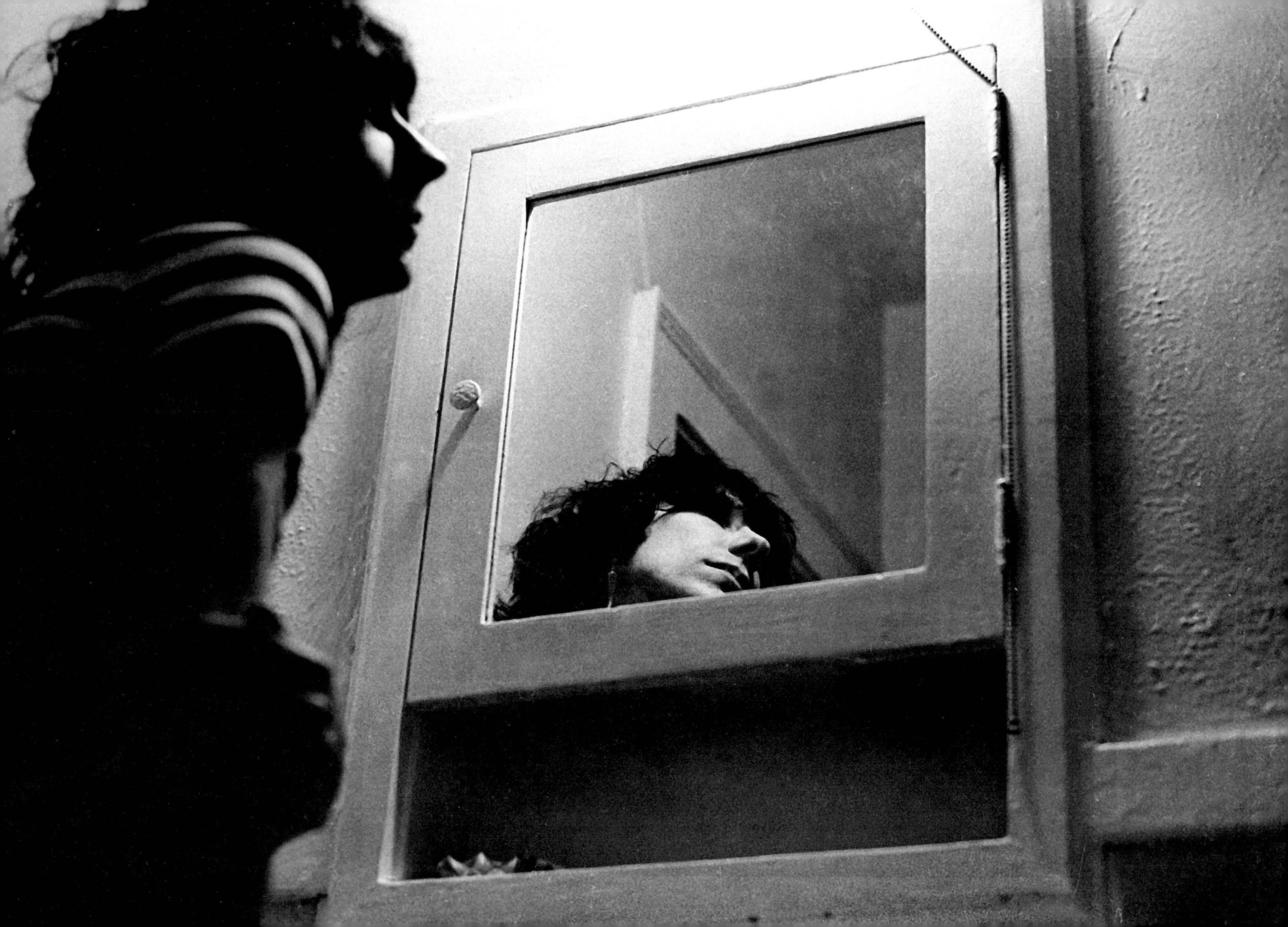

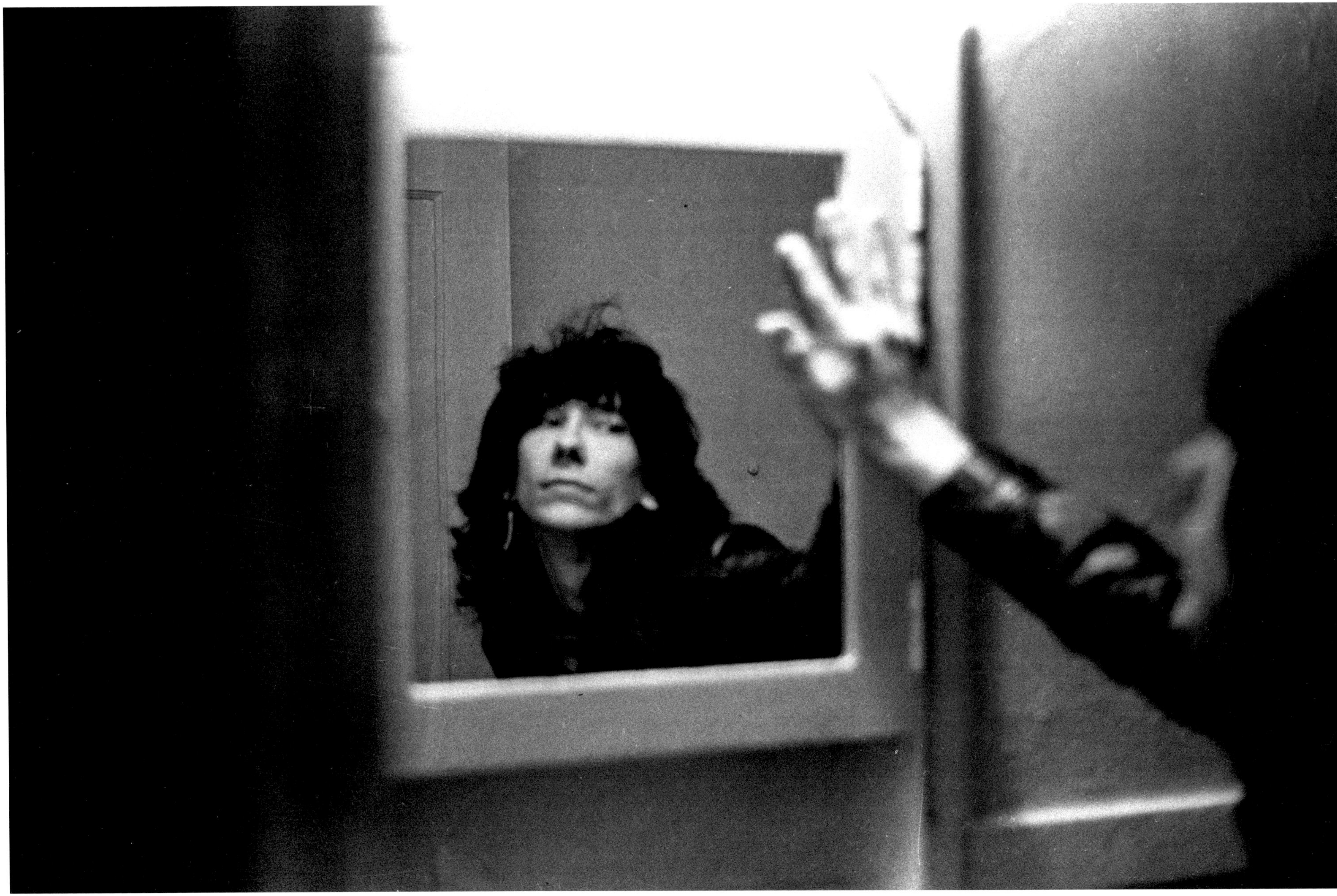

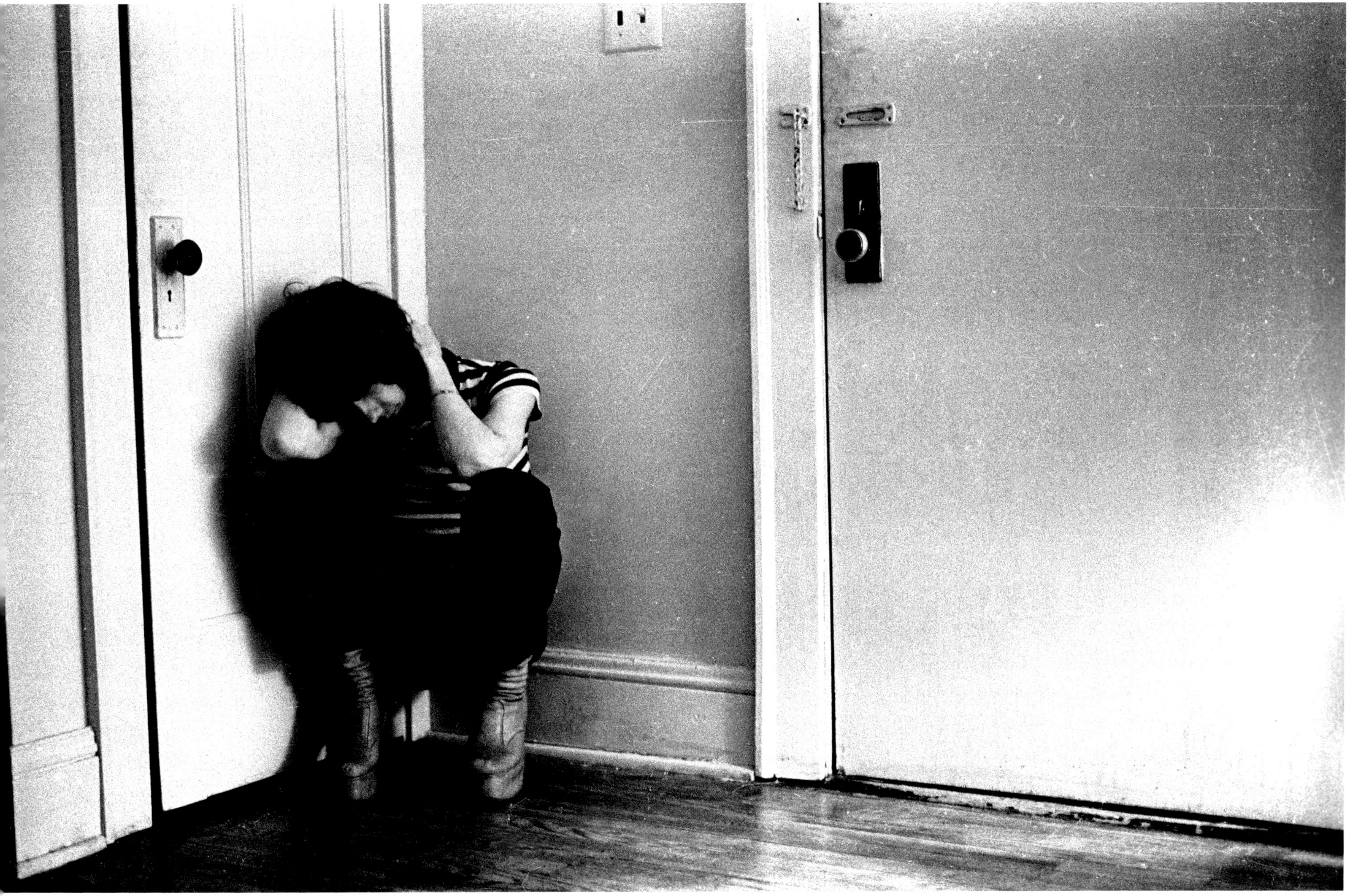

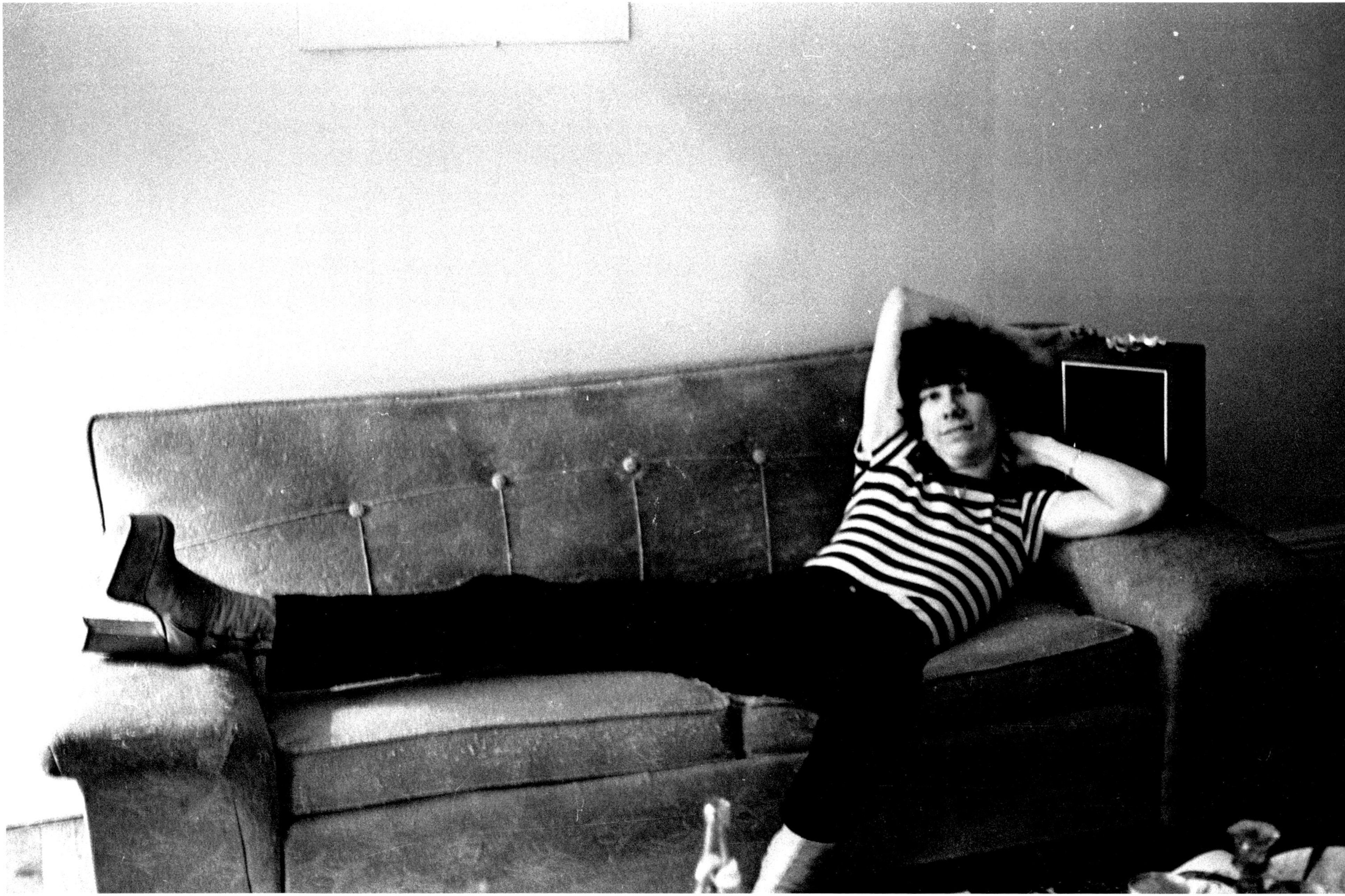

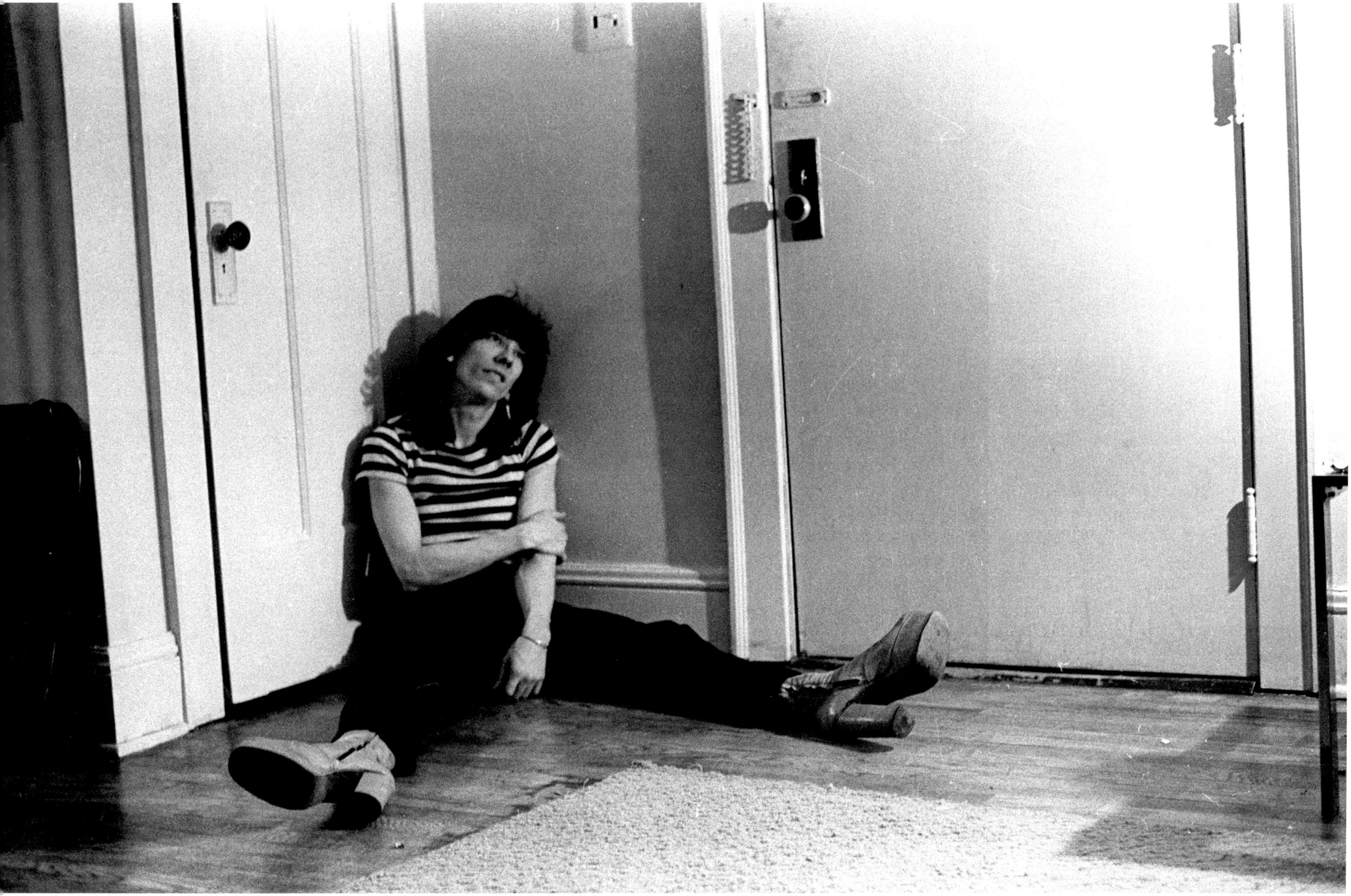

Johnny Blitz:

Those shoes—these are early shots! We were still on a Mott the Hoople kick. We weren't totally transitioned into the "punk" thing, whatever that was. There's still remnants of a glam rock phase here. By the time we got to New York those kinds of clothes were all gone, which was fine with me, I never liked that anyway. I liked the *music* though.

Cheetah Chrome:

We were big Alice Cooper, New York Dolls, and Stooges fans. Glam was the style of the time—good luck finding a pair of shoes that *didn't* have platforms back then, you know? It was either that or Converse. I always hated them, I'd rather wear sneakers than platforms, but I ended up getting a pair eventually. And the shoes Stiv's wearing in these pictures, I think were given to him by Johnny Thunders. Stiv and Jimmy were always the stylish ones, I was more of a street kid, I just wanted to wear my motorcycle jacket, jeans, and tennis shoes.

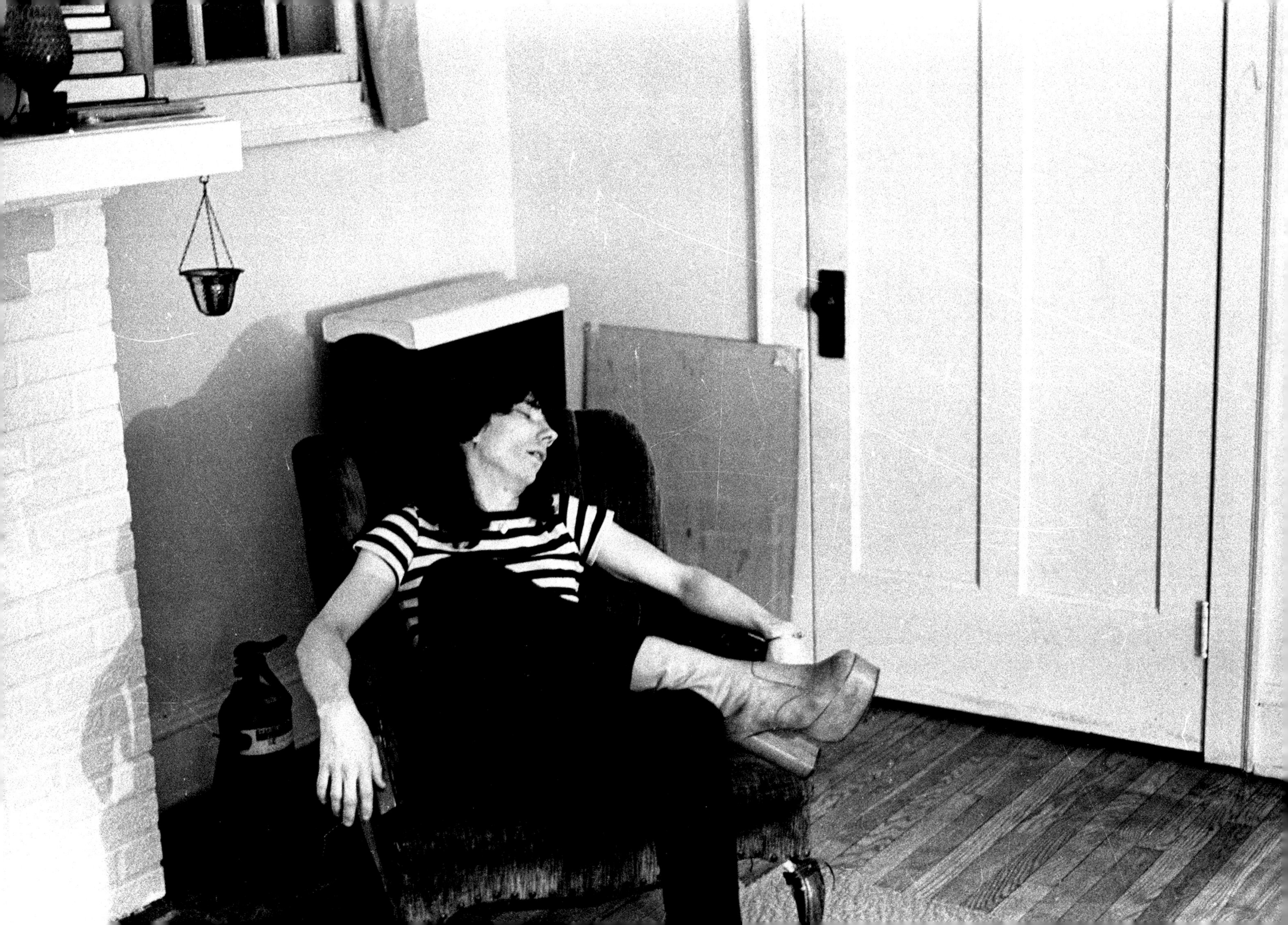

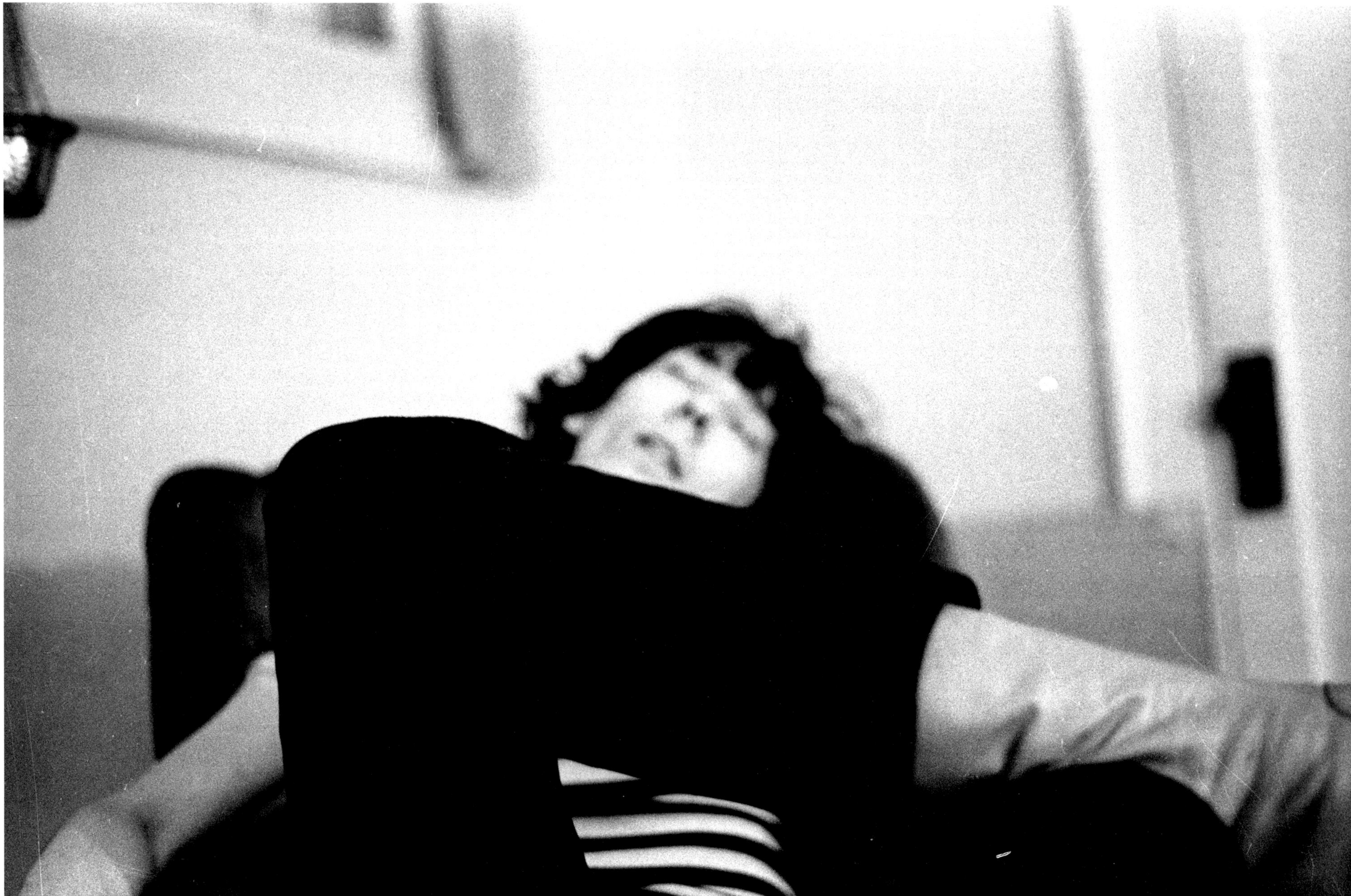

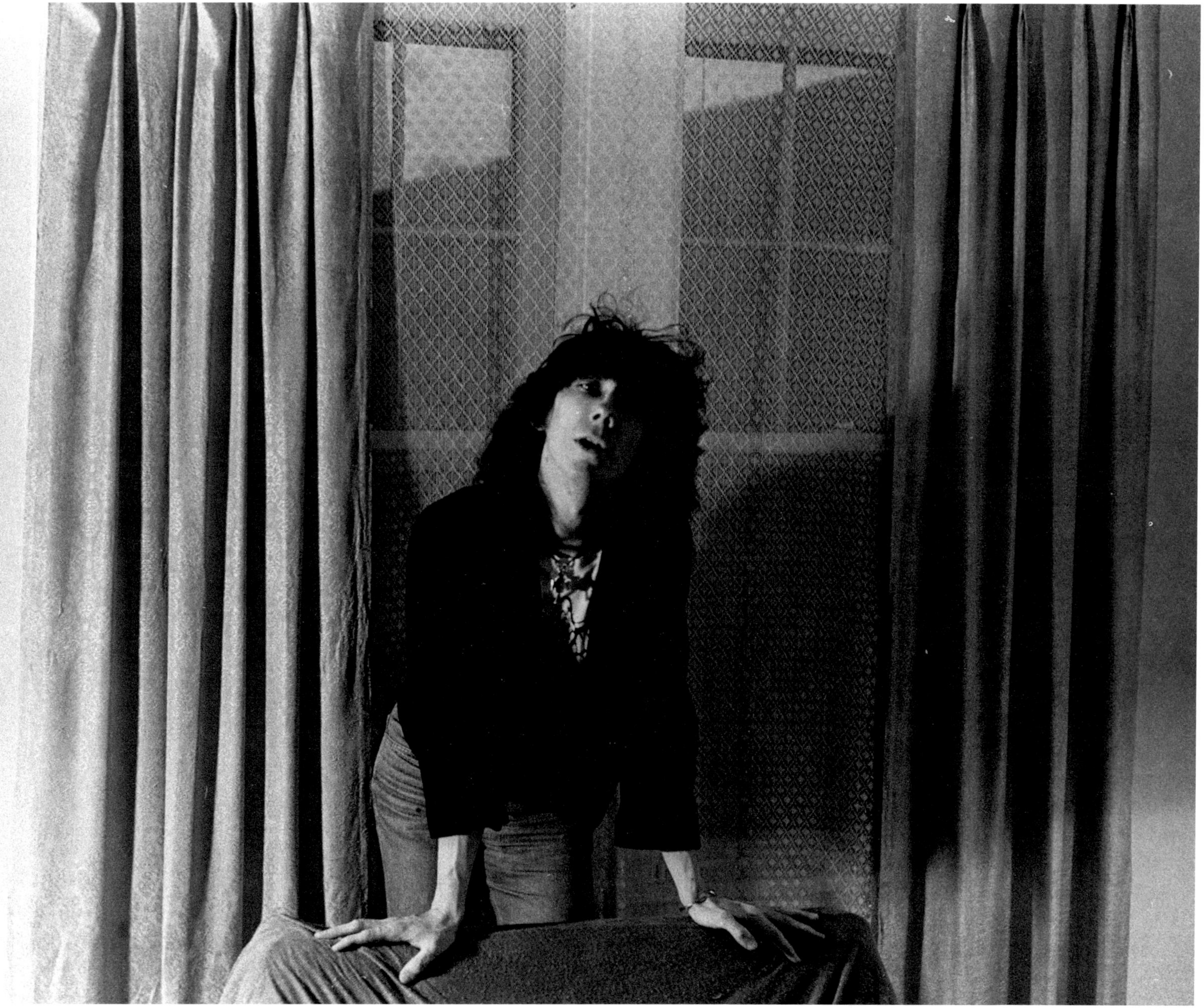

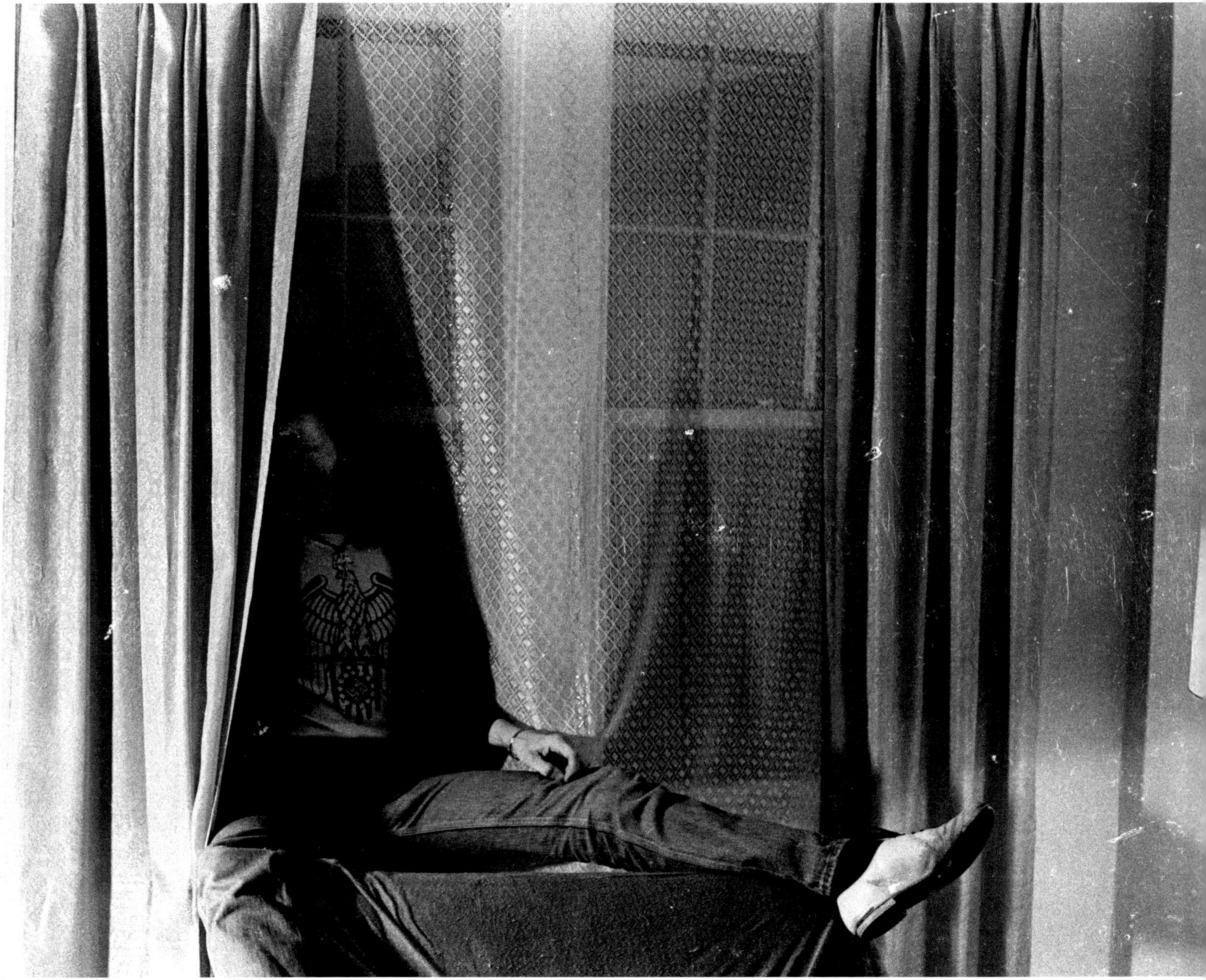

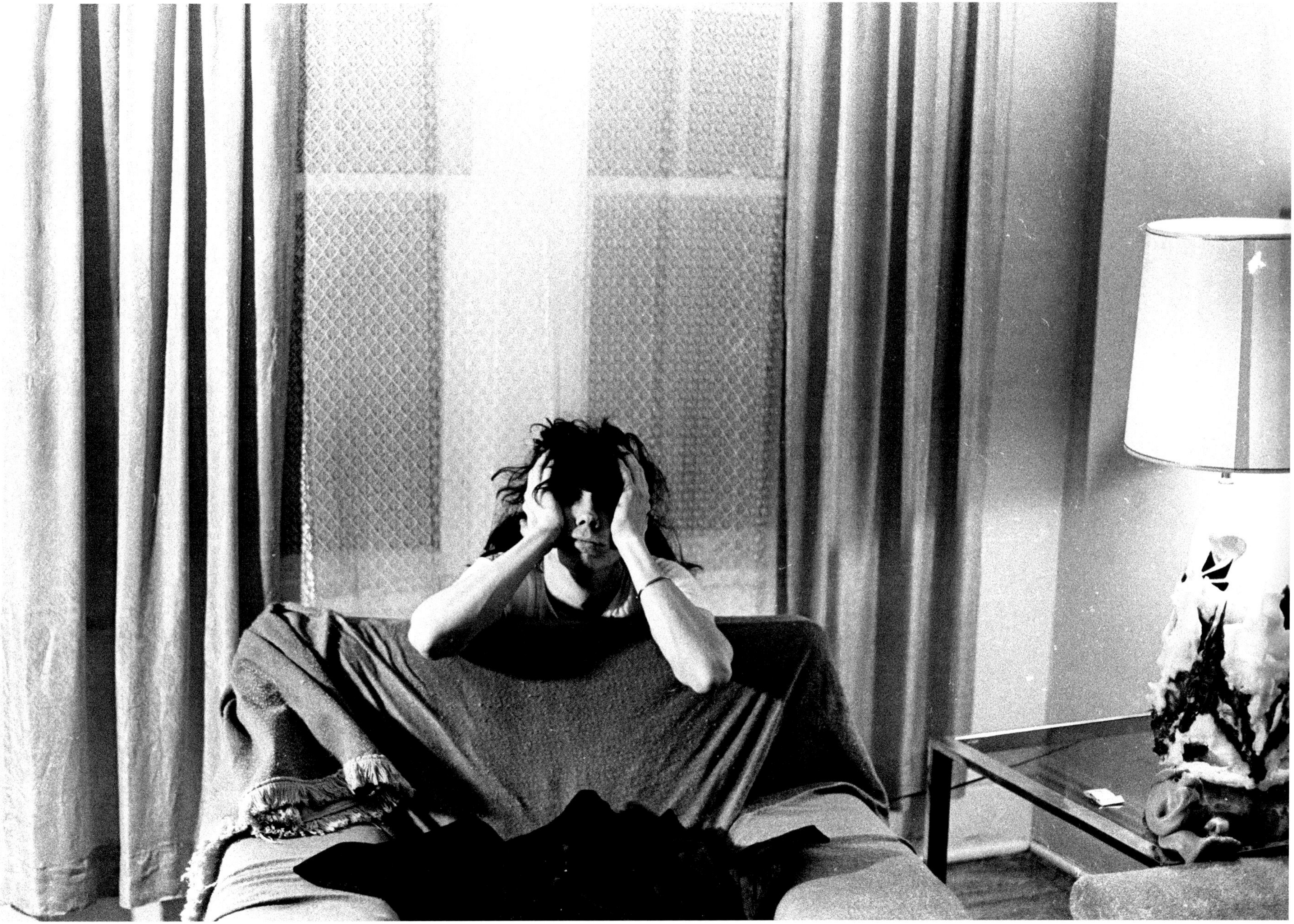

Cheetah Chrome:

There was a period when Frankenstein re-formed as the Dead Boys where me and Stiv lived in that apartment and wrote songs. It was on Giel, near Detroit Avenue in Lakewood, right by Saint Edward's [a Catholic boys' school]. I've got a scar under my eye from when we got in a fight with some St. Ed's football guys. We would open the door stark naked to Jehovah's Witnesses, I used to moon out the window, piss out the window.

We wrote music in the bathroom because it had the best acoustics, and I would use a 12-acoustic guitar to work out our songs. So we would go in there at 7:30 every night, drin smoke pot, write songs in the bathroom, and come out at 11. I think "Not Anymor "Ain't Nothin' to Do" got worked out in that bathroom. And I think "Calling on You the second album was written in there. For "High Tension Wire" I worked out my p there. But that bathroom was our work place.

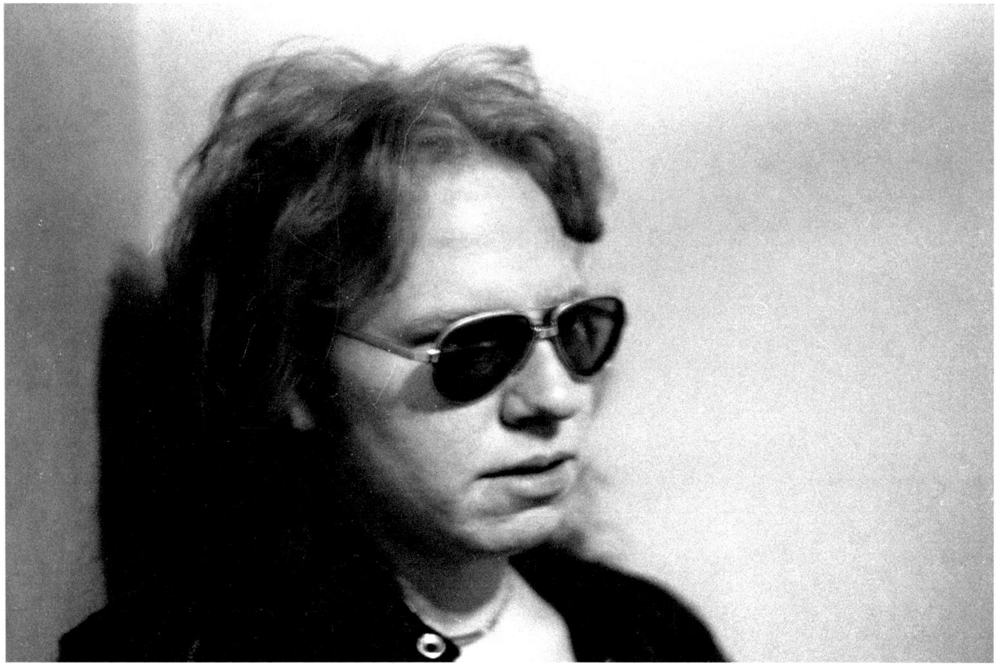

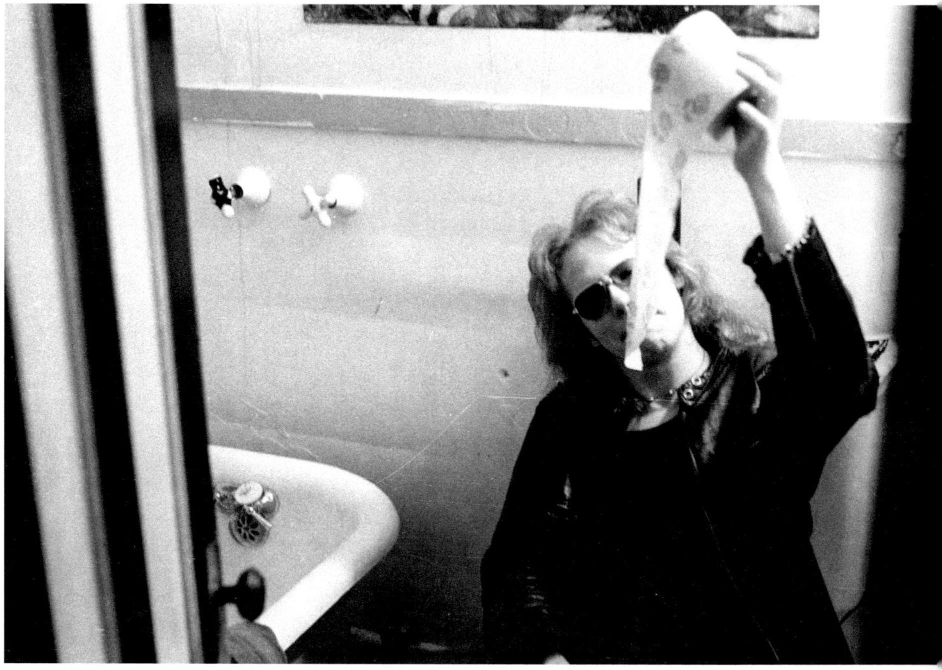

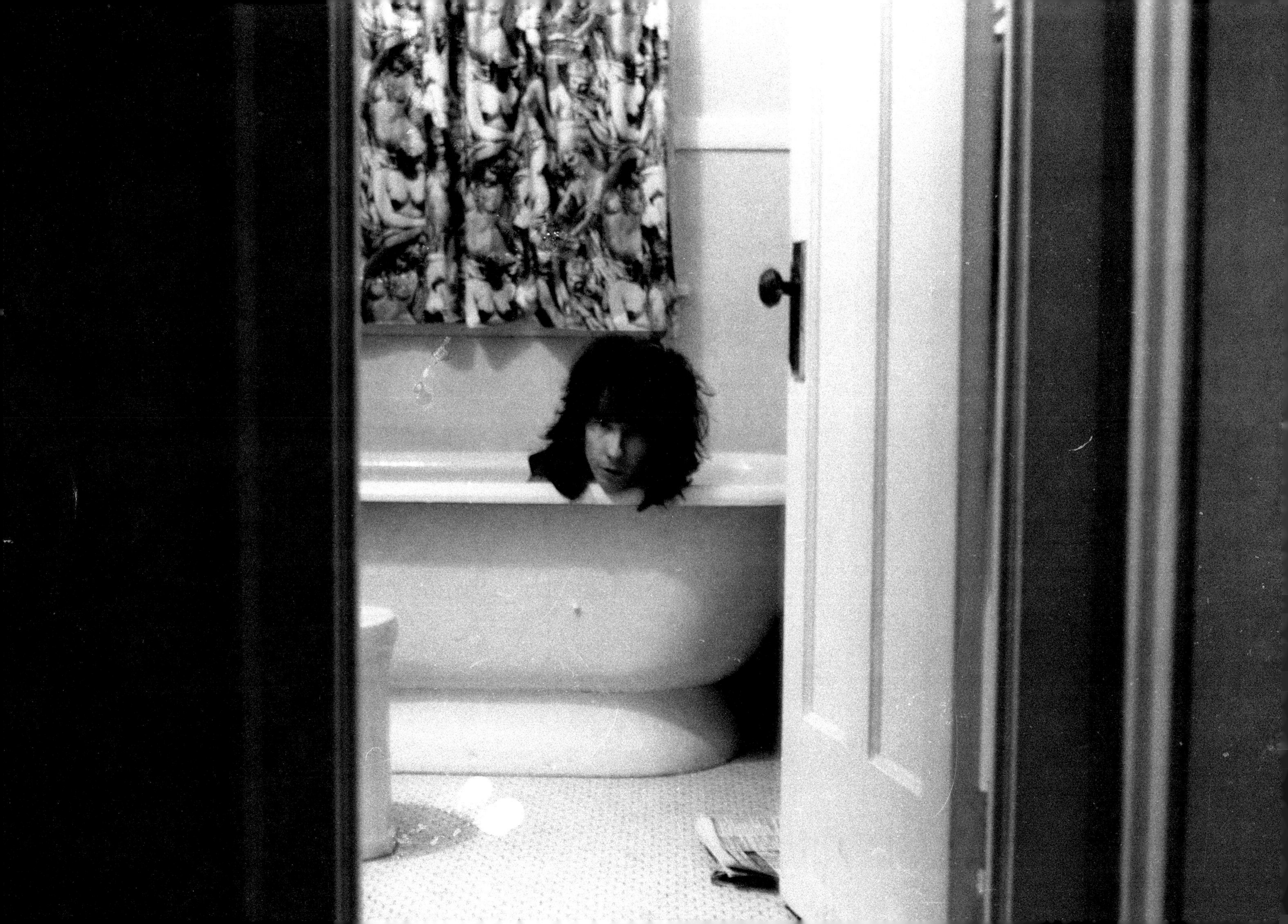

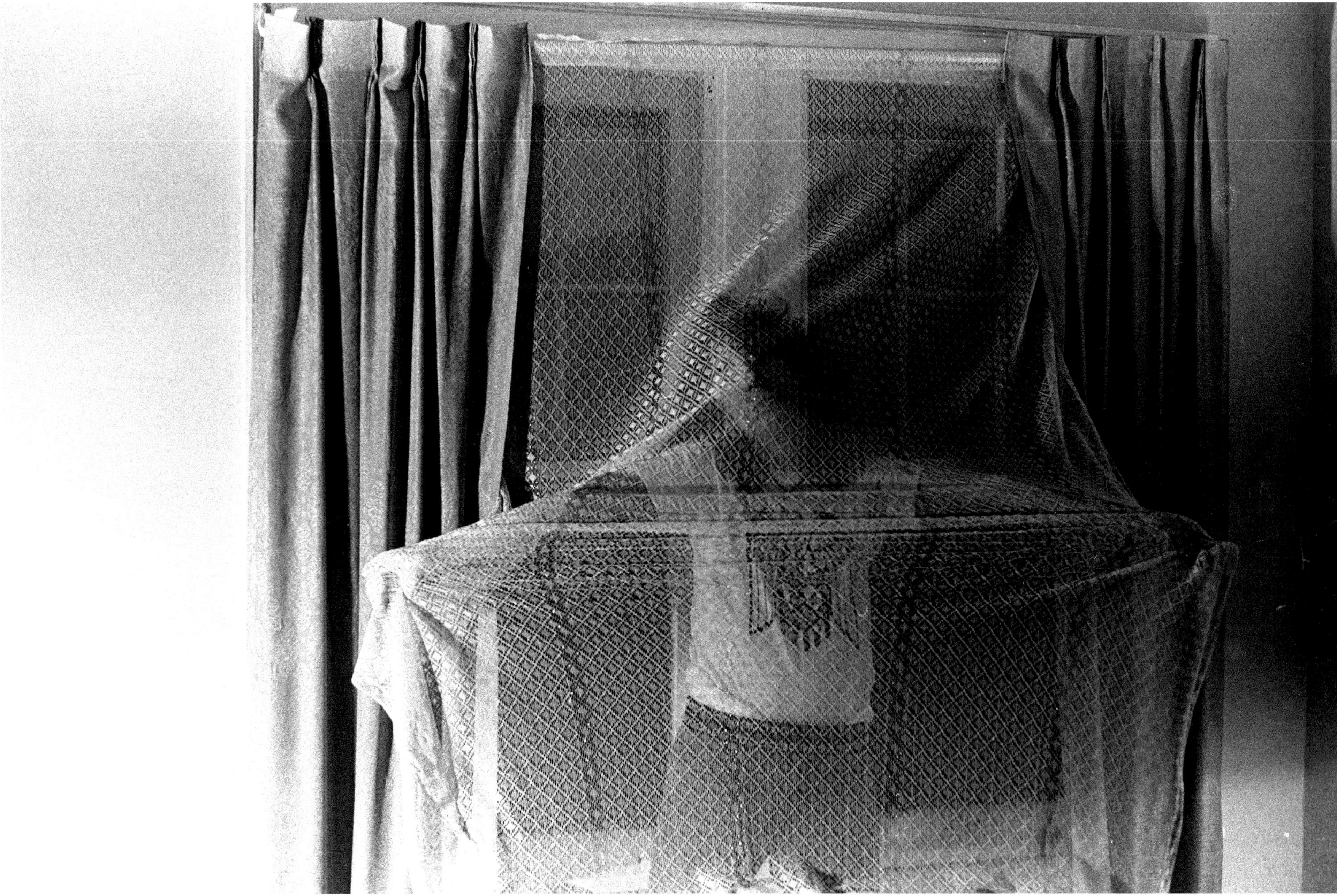

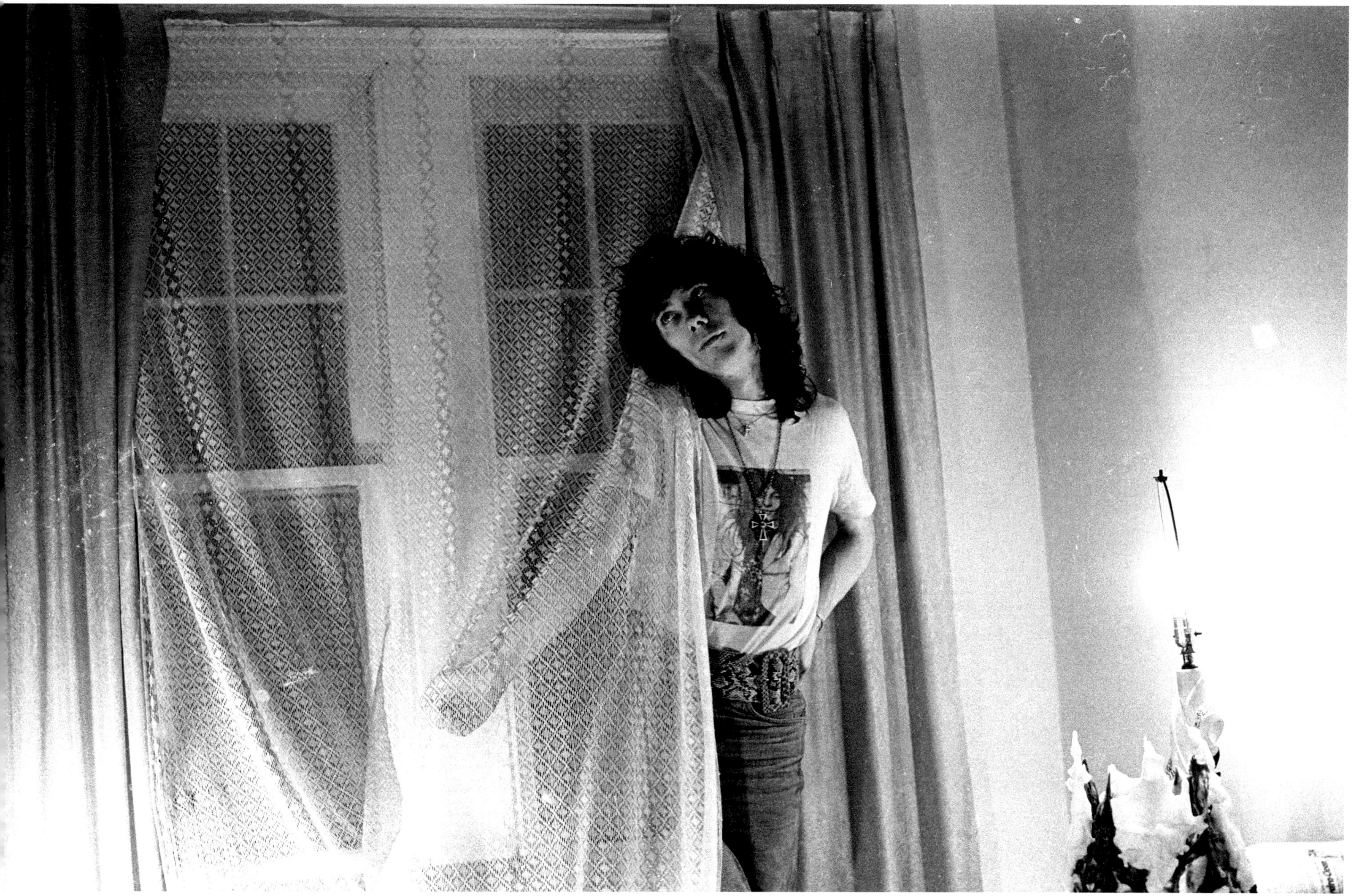

Johnny Blitz:

In 1990 I got a call from France, where Stiv was living, and I thought "OK, I guess we're going back out on the road." But it was Bators' girlfriend telling me he was hit by a car and he was dead. That was the worst day of my life, it was fucked, it was awful. We spent a lot of time together, him and I. It was like losing a member of my family, it took me years to get over it. You can't replace a guy like him, he was definitely special.

Cheetah Chrome:

I woke up with a bad hangover because I'd been out the night before at the Continental. John Spacely was ringing my doorbell, and he took me out and bought me some double and triple shots, and after a while I realized "Look, something's wrong here, who died?" I thought it was my mom, mom was in her '80s at the time, and he said "Stiv." That was how I found out. It was a good thing he bought me some shots first, because that was the last thing I was expecting.

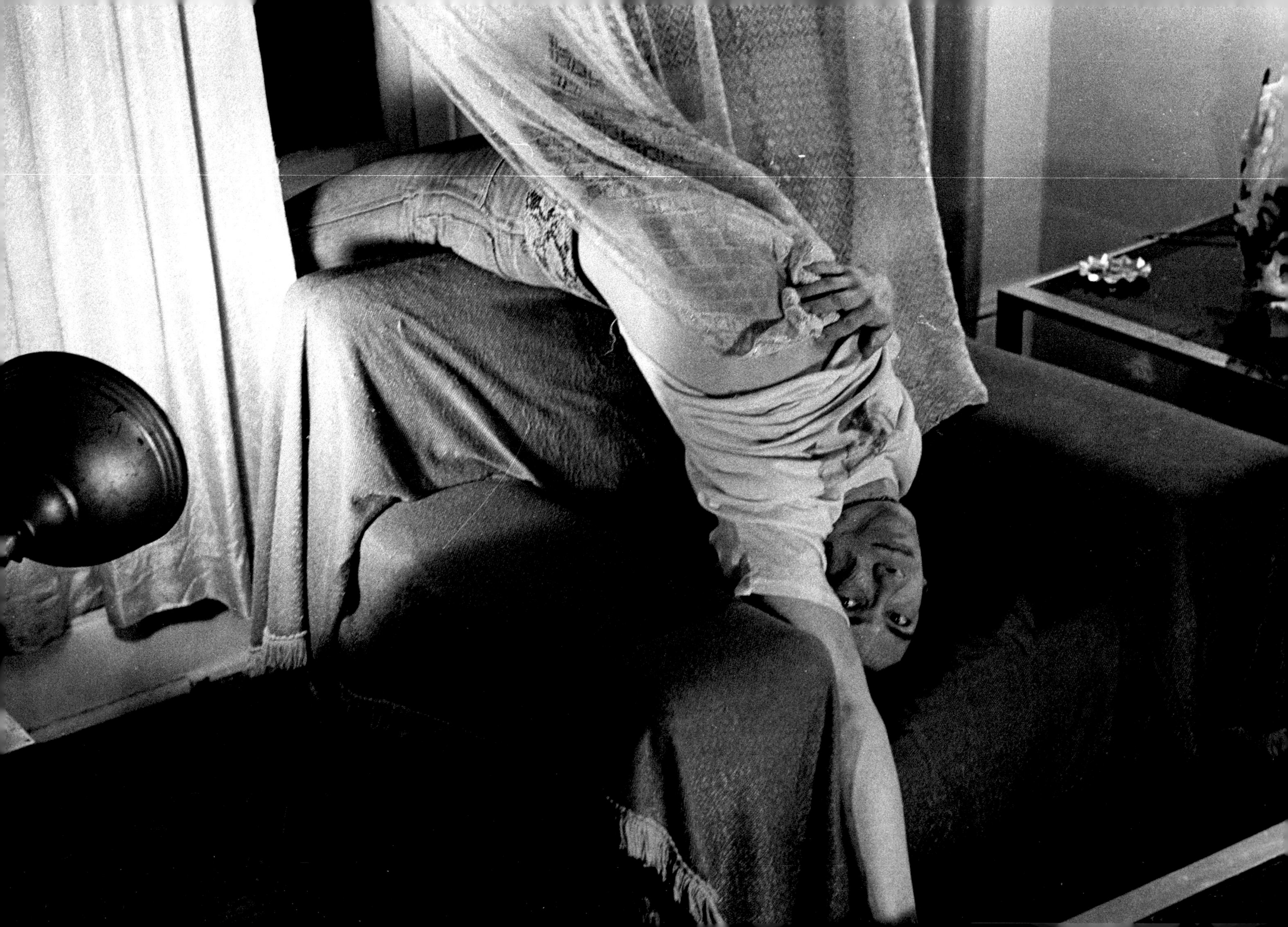

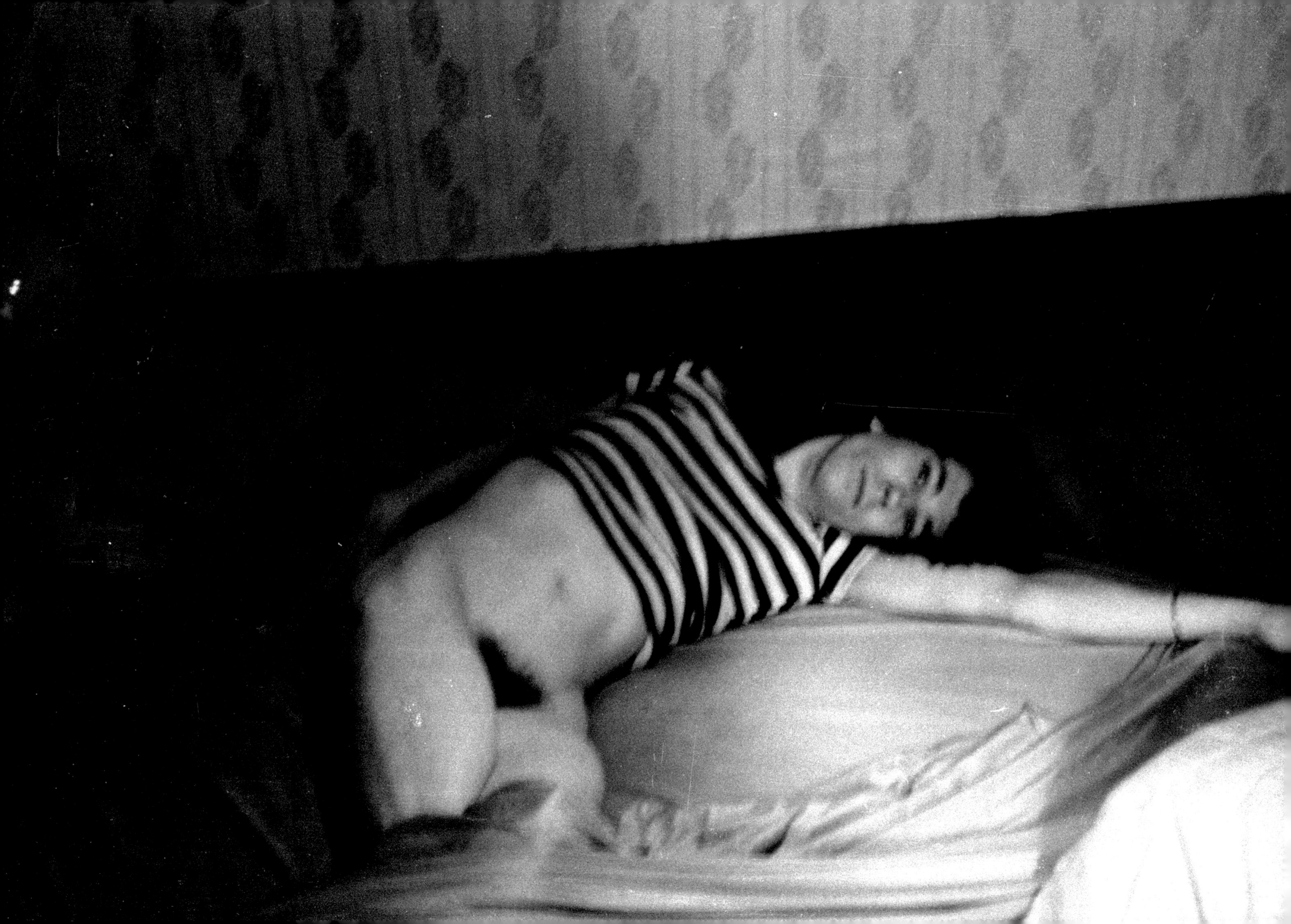